SECRET ARMIES

Resistance Groups in World War Two

Tim Healey

Macdonald

ECCO il NEMICO

CONTENTS

The author wishes to thank Harry Rée for kindly agreeing to read the text.

Far left: **An Allied anti-Nazi poster of World War II. The Italian lettering means** *This is the enemy.*

Top left: **Partisans laying explosives on a railway line in Russia.**

Centre left: **Weapons training in a Danish resistance group.**

Bottom left: **A Danish radio operator working a transmitter from inside an internment camp.**

BLITZKRIEG

The outbreak of war

In 1938, German troops marched into Austria and claimed it for the German *Reich* (empire). This action had been ordered by Adolf Hitler, Germany's Nazi leader. It was the first stage of his plan to make Germany the ruler of Europe.

Soon afterwards, Hitler demanded the Sudetenland, a border region of Czechoslovakia. Hoping to avoid a widespread war, the major European powers agreed to his demand and the Sudetenland was granted to Germany. Then, in March 1939, German troops occupied Prague, the Czech capital. The country was partitioned and ceased to exist as a nation.

Still Hitler's ambitions were not satisfied. On 1 September 1939, German troops invaded Poland. Britain and France had a treaty with Poland and now declared war on Germany. World War Two began.

Germany's early victories were dramatic. In a shattering series of *Blitzkriegs* (lightning wars) her troops smashed through Poland, Denmark, Norway, Belgium, Holland and Luxembourg.

Supported by tanks and aerial bombardment, German troops swept all before them. In June 1940, at Dunkirk, the British were forced to withdraw their troops from Europe. France fell in the same month.

Hitler wanted to invade Britain too, and only abandoned this idea when his airforce was fought off by the Royal Air Force in the Battle of Britain (July–October 1940). But German conquests went on. The following year Hitler occupied Yugoslavia and Greece.

The invasion of Russia

The Germans did not act alone. Italy, Finland, Hungary, Rumania and Bulgaria co-operated with them. But Hitler's real strength had been a peace pact with the Soviet Union. Communist Russia had not threatened him.

Then, in June 1941, Hitler broke the pact and ordered the invasion of Russia. At first, blitzkrieg tactics brought success and by December 1941 the Germans had almost reached Moscow.

But there they were checked. In the same month, Hitler declared war on the United States. With the two giants of Russia and the United States now ranged against him, the course of the war slowly changed. But Europe remained under the Nazi jackboot.

Above: **A Dutch cartoon which shows Europe ravaged by the Nazi leaders: Goering (airforce chief), Hitler, and Goebbels (the head of Nazi propaganda).**

Right: **Map showing Hitler's Europe at the height of Nazi power. The occupied capitals are marked by the swastika, symbol of the Nazi party.**

Below: **German troops fighting in Russia, where the Blitzkrieg advance was checked.**

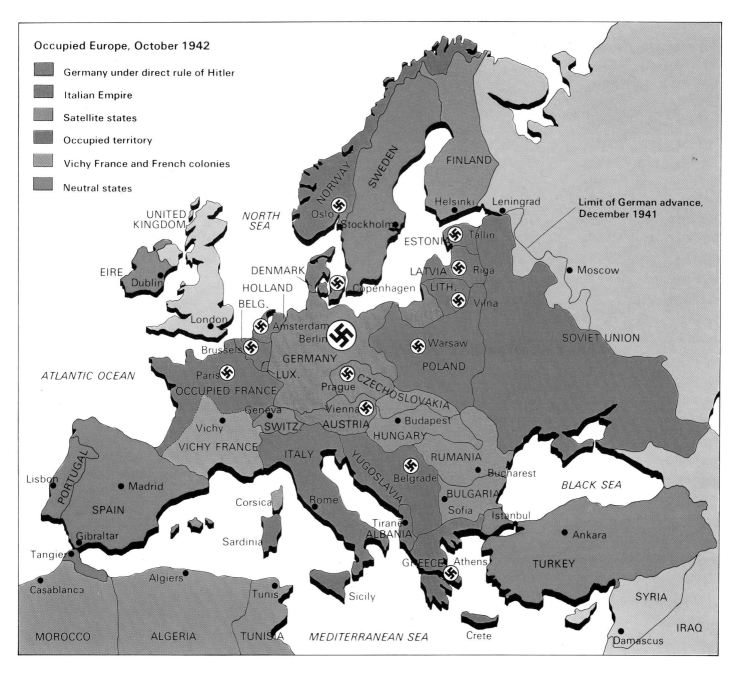

Occupied Europe, October 1942

- Germany under direct rule of Hitler
- Italian Empire
- Satellite states
- Occupied territory
- Vichy France and French colonies
- Neutral states

Limit of German advance, December 1941

Hitler's Europe

In Hitler's Europe, only Switzerland, Sweden, Spain and Portugal remained neutral states. The rest were either occupied by the Germans or controlled by their allies and satellites (states which took orders from Germany).

Conditions varied in the occupied countries. Many of the worst repressions occurred in the East, in Russia and Poland, where the Nazis planned to gain *Lebensraum* (living space) for the German people. Here the inhabitants were treated as inferior beings. Jews were persecuted on a terrifying scale.

In the West, Hitler hoped to win co-operation from the conquered peoples. At first, German troops behaved well and the persecution of particular groups such as the Jews began more slowly.

In Denmark, Hitler even permitted an election (however, the local Nazi party only won two per cent of the vote so the experiment was not repeated).

Collaborators

In most places the Nazis governed through local collaborators (people who willingly co-operated with them). For example, the Norwegian, Vidkun Quisling, ruled his country as a dictator on Germany's behalf. Thereafter, collaborators were referred to as 'quislings'.

The government of France was split. The Germans occupied the north, declaring the whole Atlantic coast a forbidden zone. But in the south, a new French government was set up, based in the town of Vichy. It was headed by Marshal Pétain, a hero of World War One.

The Germans did not occupy 'Vichy France', but Pétain's government did collaborate with them. And when the Allies invaded North Africa in late 1942, the Germans were able to take over Vichy France without serious opposition.

The shock of defeat

During the first two years of war it took exceptional courage to offer active resistance to the Germans. The conquered peoples were stunned by the collapse of their armies, and felt bitter and bewildered.

In France, many people even admired Pétain. They were thankful that he had come to terms with the Germans quickly and avoided a long struggle which could have destroyed France. At this stage, Nazi Germany seemed invincible.

5

OCCUPATION

Daily life

Daily life under the Occupation was drab. The Germans seized the best local produce for themselves, so food, fuel and clothing had to be rationed. German officers ate in the good restaurants, while local people drank coffee made from acorns, with powdered milk and saccharine instead of sugar. Food could generally be obtained somehow in country areas, but townspeople often went hungry.

A flourishing 'black market' grew up. Rationed goods were sold illegally at many times their pre-war prices.

There were few cars on the streets, for petrol was scarce. In Paris, motor taxis were replaced by *velo taxis*: pedal bikes with sidecars.

The Germans imposed curfews at night. Anyone seen on the streets after a certain hour could be arrested. Movement was restricted, with train inspections and spot checks in the street.

At first, most people simply put up with these miseries. But a spirit of passive resistance was always present.

In Holland, bars and cafés would fall silent if a German entered. Customers just drank up and left. In Denmark, King Christian waved to his people in the streets. But he would not acknowledge a German salute. He attended a service in a synagogue to protest against the persecution of Jews.

In Norway, Quisling tried to get history taught from the Nazi viewpoint. Every history teacher refused and every one was imprisoned. Then he tried to make the teachers join a political union. Almost all refused. The schools closed, and only opened again when Quisling backed down.

The Nazis needed people to work in German farms and factories, since most young Germans were doing military service. Hitler first called for volunteers from the conquered nations to work in Germany. Later he made labour service compulsory. To avoid it, thousands of young men went into hiding.

Above: **German troops parade beneath the Arc de Triomphe in Paris. The Nazi flag hung from public buildings in the French capital, as a humiliating reminder of defeat.**

Below: **A civilian being questioned by a night-time police patrol in Denmark. Police forces in the occupied countries were required to work with the Germans.**

MARCHÉ
NOIR
CRIME CONTRE LA COMMUNAUTÉ

Dawn of resistance

From mid 1940 to mid 1941 Britain and her Commonwealth allies stood almost alone against Germany. But national leaders from many of the defeated countries had managed to escape to London where they set up 'governments-in-exile' as rivals to the German quislings.

Hundreds of servicemen escaped too, and formed their own units to fight alongside the British. (Dutch and Polish airmen fought in the Battle of Britain, for example.) These forces were known as the Allies, and many families inside occupied Europe had members fighting in the Allied ranks.

A young French general called Charles de Gaulle was one of the first to rally the forces of resistance in Europe. He had been a little-known tank commander and reached England after the fall of France.

In a BBC broadcast on 18 June 1940, de Gaulle called on all loyal Frenchmen to continue the struggle. 'Whatever happens,' he declared, 'the flame of French resistance must not be quenched and will not be quenched.'

De Gaulle set up a Free French Army and formed an intelligence service working into occupied France.

When Russia entered the war, active resistance increased because Communists throughout Europe threw themselves into the struggle. Many were already disciplined and skilled in secret warfare.

Further hope came when the United States entered the war, and the Resistance movement grew rapidly.

Active resistance took three main forms: spying, escape work and subversion (a broad term covering propaganda, sabotage and armed attacks).

The people involved ranged from shop assistants to millionaires. Most resisters were very ordinary people who took on extraordinary work with no particular skill or training. And the dangers they faced were also extraordinary, for unlike servicemen they could expect no mercy if they were captured.

They knew the risks they were taking. Hundreds were to meet torture and death, and hundreds more faced the nightmare of the concentration camps.

A few resisters enjoyed the excitement of the secret war. But many more were sick with fear as they carried out their work. This makes their courage all the more striking, their sacrifices all the more moving.

Above: A French poster warns that the black market is a 'crime against the community'. Country people made good money by hoarding food and selling it illegally to hungry townspeople. Townspeople were prepared to pay high prices for it—it was one way of beating the German system.

Right: A poster encouraging people to go and do labour service in Germany. Those who accepted faced hard work under miserable conditions. During the second half of 1942, all Frenchmen of military age became liable for compulsory labour service, and widespread resistance began.

Left: A selection of the personal papers needed under the Occupation. They include identity cards, travel permits and ration coupons. Getting hold of real documents from which to make forgeries was one of the first tasks of the Allied intelligence agencies.

EN TRAVAILLANT EN ALLEMAGNE
tu seras l'Ambassadeur de la
QUALITÉ FRANÇAISE

THE NAZI TERROR

Against the Resistance

The Germans described resisters as 'terrorists' and dealt with them through several official bodies.

The *Abwehr* was Germany's regular army security and intelligence organization. It had a secret police force whose agents often worked in plain clothes.

The Abwehr had existed before the Nazis came to power in Germany, and its officers did not usually behave as barbarously as Nazis. They often despised the Nazis and even obstructed their work.

The Abwehr's two main rivals were the *Gestapo* (state police) and *SD* (security service). Both of these were Nazi party organizations and their officers were members of the *SS* (protection squad).

The SS itself had begun as Hitler's personal bodyguard. But the organization had swelled enormously by the beginning of the war. It developed its own factories and its own armed force, the *Waffen SS*, into which thousands of collaborators were recruited. The SS had another grim function. Its members ran the Nazi concentration camps.

Obviously, there was nothing specially wicked about the Germans. The evils of the Occupation lay in the Nazi system. Many atrocities were committed by collaborators, acting against their own people. For example, the Frenchman Joseph Darnand headed a right-wing Militia which had 45,000 members. They could be just as vicious as any German Gestapo agent—and even more dangerous.

Above: **Enemies of the Resistance:**

Heinrich Himmler (left) was the German head of the SS. As such, he was the chief of all the forces working against the Resistance.

Reinhard Heydrich (right) was his second-in-command. He was made governor of German occupied Czechoslovakia in September 1941. His assassination led to the reprisals at Lidice.

Right: **An American poster describes the horror of Lidice. A chained and hooded victim is used to symbolize Nazi brutality.**

The atrocity was carried out on the direct orders of Hitler. The village was destroyed, and the rubble ploughed into the ground. Even the name of Lidice was removed from maps.

This is Nazi brutality

RADIO BERLIN.--IT IS OFFICIALLY ANNOUNCED:-
ALL MEN OF LIDICE - CZECHOSLOVAKIA - HAVE BEEN SHOT:
THE WOMEN DEPORTED TO A CONCENTRATION CAMP:
THE CHILDREN SENT TO APPROPRIATE CENTERS-- THE
NAME OF THE VILLAGE WAS IMMEDIATELY ABOLISHED.
6/11/42/115P

Left: **A Gestapo thumbscrew. Other methods of torture included head vices and electric shock treatment. In the dungeons at Breendonk in Belgium, the Belgian SS set starving dogs on their victims. One of the SS greeted new arrivals with the words: 'This is hell and I am the devil.'**

Right: **The uniform of a member of the Dutch WA (a branch of Holland's NSB, the local Nazi party). Collaborators maintained the Nazi terror in occupied Europe. Holland was governed internally by ten leading NSB officials. Three of them were assassinated by resisters in 1943.**

Below: **SS troops round up a group of partisans in Russia. Under Hitler's 'Nacht und Nebel' (Night and Fog) decree of December 1941, 'enemies of the Reich' could be interrogated by any methods, and executed without trial. Partisans like these would be shot or hung within hours of their arrest.**

Interrogation

The collaborators knew the resister's language and neighbourhood. They were more likely to spot anything unusual, and less likely to be fooled during an interrogation. Bodies like the Militia worked closely with the Gestapo. They were hated, not only as enemies, but as traitors.

Local police forces were also supposed to be working with the Germans. However, many members secretly aided the Resistance.

The Nazis and their sympathizers used methods of ferocious brutality. Interrogation often involved torture. Whippings and beatings were almost routine, while another common method was to half-drown a suspect in a bath of icy water, then question the gasping victim.

Even the bravest resisters could not guarantee to keep silent under torture. They generally tried to hold out for 48 hours, giving their friends time to discover the arrest and flee.

The Lidice massacre

As the war dragged on, armed attacks by civilians on the Germans increased, and mass reprisals were taken. Fifty or more civilians might be executed for one dead German soldier. Reprisals were particularly savage against the peoples of Eastern Europe.

In May 1942, Czechoslovakia was ruled by an SS officer, Reinhard Heydrich. Two Czech agents, trained by the British, ambushed him as he was being driven home from his office. Heydrich was wounded and died later in hospital.

The assassins committed suicide after a gun battle with the SS. But their deaths did not satisfy the Nazis. Another agent, unconnected with the attack, was captured and found to be carrying a note which mentioned the village of Lidice.

This evidence was enough for the SS. All the male population of Lidice and its neighbouring village, Lezaky, were shot: 197 people. The women and children were deported or sent to concentration camps. Hundreds of Czech prisoners in Nazi gaols were murdered. Altogether, more than 2000 people were slaughtered.

The atrocity was a blow from which the Czech Resistance never fully recovered. But reprisals did not always put an end to armed attacks. On the contrary, they often made people even more determined to resist.

PROPAGANDA

Broadcasting

The Nazis devoted immense energy to propaganda. Posters portrayed cheerful German soldiers as friends, while Jews, Communists and Allied leaders were depicted as villains.

The Nazis controlled the radio and newspapers. They thundered constant news of German successes to discourage all thoughts of resistance. In the early days of defeat it was vital for the Allies to counter-attack.

News and rallying speeches by exiled leaders were broadcast on the foreign service of the BBC. There were lighter touches too, in the witty *Les Français Parlent aux Français* (The French Speak to the French) which included songs, jingles and short plays.

Programmes like this were immensely popular in occupied Europe, and listening to the BBC was a serious offence. But with curtains drawn and the volume low, even timid resisters tuned in.

Radio Moscow and neutral Swiss and Swedish radio broadcasts could also be heard in some areas. Though the Nazis tried to jam foreign transmissions, they never succeeded completely.

The underground press

Inside occupied Europe itself, secret printing presses produced thousands of pamphlets and underground newspapers. Some were just smudged broadsheets with snippets of news gleaned from Allied broadcasts. Others were highly professional productions (one French paper had a circulation of half a million by 1944).

Many of the leading writers of the day contributed articles: for example, Sartre, Camus, Malraux and de Beauvoir in France. Their quality proved that resisters were not mere 'terrorists'. When the contributors to Denmark's *Frit Danmark* were arrested, they were found to include many of the country's foremost figures in literature, law and medicine.

Hundreds of illegal presses were set up in hidden cellars. But the larger papers often used legal printing presses which were turned over to the Resistance at night.

Distributing underground newspapers was dangerous, and the penalties could be just as severe as for spying or sabotage. Many heroes of the Resistance began their work in this field.

Below left: **a German poster invites Norwegians to fight in the Waffen SS presenting them as the Norsemen of old.**

Below right: **poster showing Holland's exiled queen, Wilhelmina, who broadcast on the BBC in the Allied cause.**

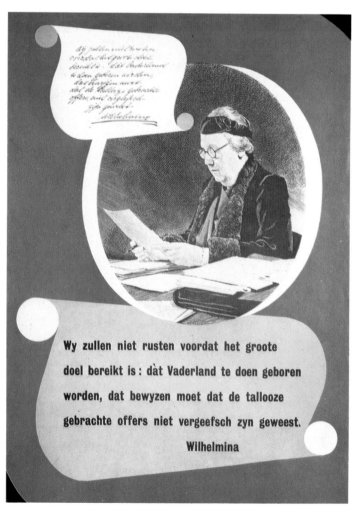

Propaganda campaigns

The Allies set up special agencies to wage propaganda warfare. Their planes showered hundreds of tonnes of leaflets on occupied Europe during the war.

Their work also involved spreading 'black' propaganda, that is, false information designed to confuse and demoralize the enemy. For example, they printed fake German news sheets giving the wrong orders, and fake currency and ration cards to disrupt the Nazi economy.

Handbooks explaining how to feign illness were dropped by plane for use by malingering soldiers and workers wanting to avoid labour service. Black radio stations were set up. The broadcasters pretended to be loyal Germans, while spreading false rumours about Nazi officials.

It is hard to know what effect black propaganda had. But the results of another campaign were visible everywhere: using V as a symbol of resistance.

This was first suggested on the BBC's Belgian programme in 1941. 'V' stood for *Victoire* (Victory) in French, and *Vriejheid* (Freedom) in Flemish, the two languages spoken in Belgium.

Above: **A secret press printing an underground paper in Denmark.**

Right: **An issue of the French underground paper, 'Combat'.**

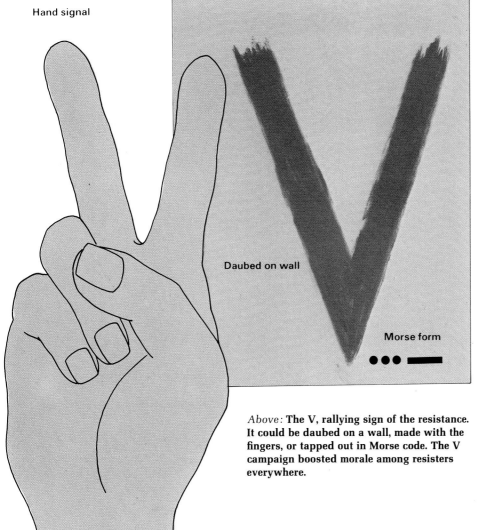

Hand signal

Daubed on wall

Morse form

Above: **The V, rallying sign of the resistance. It could be daubed on a wall, made with the fingers, or tapped out in Morse code. The V campaign boosted morale among resisters everywhere.**

The V campaign

The V campaign soon swept occupied Europe. The V symbol appeared daubed on houses, walls and pavements. It was chalked overnight on German trucks and even on German military headquarters. Some towns became a mass of V symbols. In Belgium itself it was said that 'never has so much chalk been sold'.

The campaign was developed. The British Prime Minister, Winston Churchill made the V symbol with his fingers as a sign of encouragement and it was soon picked up by Allied troops.

The Morse code form for V (three short taps and one long one) echoed the first notes in Beethoven's Fifth Symphony. They were used at the beginning of BBC foreign service broadcasts. The tune could be whistled in the street under the very noses of the occupiers.

Eventually, the Germans started to use the V symbol themselves to celebrate their own victories. The hectic V campaign slowed down.

But the V remained an international rallying sign. When the oppressed peoples of Europe saw it chalked on walls or buildings, they knew that the Resistance was among them.

THE HIDDEN EYES

Spies

Gathering intelligence (information) was an important task for the Resistance. The Allies intended to liberate Europe one day, so it was vital for them to know the number and strength of German units in every region. Advance knowledge of enemy intentions was also essential, and information about German factories and airfields meant that they could be pinpointed for bombing.

For tasks like these, the Resistance could offer an army of spies. Some workers occupied particularly useful positions. Railway clerks found out what units and equipment were being sent where. Hotel porters sifted through their German visitors' luggage. Waiters could glean information by listening to careless talk among their German customers.

All ran terrible risks without even knowing what value their information might hold. The mass of reports was then smuggled out to the Allied intelligence services who fitted it all together to form an overall picture. In turn, they supplied equipment, sent in agents and pinpointed new targets for penetration.

Intelligence agencies

The British had their own Secret Intelligence Service (SIS—also known as MI 6). America's wartime secret service was called the OSS (Office of Strategic Services) and had a department dealing with espionage. Russia had two intelligence agencies, the GRU (military) and NKVD (state). The governments-in-exile also formed networks.

Above: **An RAF observer with a camera used in aerial reconnaissance. Aerial photography often picked up evidence of German defence works and secret projects. Resistance groups on the ground would then be called in to try to penetrate the sites.**

Left: **A German poster warns against speaking too freely in public places. Waiters were valuable sources of news and gossip. Both the Resistance, and the Germans, formed spy networks among the waiters in Parisian restaurants. The staff of hotels and lodging houses were good sources too.**

Right: **Two Dutch girls demonstrate the art of taking secret photographs. One has a camera hidden in her basket, and focuses on the target while pretending to fumble among her belongings. Her companion keeps lookout. Rough pencil sketches of defence works could be made in a similar way.**

Equipment

A spy's needs included cameras and film, which were banned by the Germans in sensitive areas. The Rega Minox miniature camera was particularly handy for concealment.

But most resistance networks had to work with humbler tools. They developed their own methods of secret photography. Girls snapped targets through their shopping bags. Fishermen working offshore photographed beach defences through the mesh of their nets.

More than once, resistance groups used professional safe-breakers to obtain vital documents. But sometimes, quick wits and a cool nerve alone produced dazzling results.

Above: **Tools of the spy's trade:**
The Leica 3A camera on the left could be adapted for photographing secret documents. The miniature Rega Minox is shown bottom centre, with its tiny film cassette above.
The 'Handilite' torch on the right needed no batteries. It was operated by hand-pumping the lever to generate a beam light.

The Atlantic Wall

The Germans planned to build a massive complex of defences along the Atlantic coast, against the threatened Allied invasion. Blockhouses, minefields and gun emplacements were to stretch from Norway to the Pyrenees. The fortifications were known as the Atlantic Wall and a body called the Todt Organization was responsible for building it in conditions of great secrecy.

De Gaulle's intelligence service was determined to penetrate the Wall. A huge French network called 'Century', composed of local people, began to gather information about it. One member, a house-painter called René Duchez, got himself a job decorating the office of a major in the Todt Organization.

On his very first day, Duchez noticed a large map lying on the major's desk. With a thumping heart, he took the map and slipped it behind a picture on the wall. Later, he returned and smuggled it out of the building.

When unfolded, the map was over two metres long. It was a detailed, top-secret blueprint of the Wall in Normandy.

After a series of hair-raising adventures, Century's organizer, Gilbert Renault (code-name 'Colonel Rémy') managed to smuggle the map to England on a fishing vessel. The precious map was hidden in a biscuit tin. Renault and his family escaped in the boat with it.

The map proved immensely valuable to the Allies when they eventually launched the mass invasion of Normandy on D-Day, 6 June 1944. They had known the positions of many bunkers, blockhouses and gun batteries before they had even been built.

THE INTELLIGENCE NETS

The professionals

The amateur spy networks had a very high casualty rate. This was largely because everybody knew everybody else. If one member was caught, the chances were that the others would be caught too. The less each spy knew about his or her comrades the better.

In the more professional networks, agents called 'cut-outs' were used. They acted as go-betweens, collecting information from spies in the field and passing it on to the director of the network. In this way, a spy never needed to know the identity of the director, or even of the other spies.

Cut-outs also acted as talent-spotters, seeking out useful recruits. Once contact was established, the cut-out met the agents as rarely as possible. Information was passed on at 'letter-boxes', such as a trusted tobacconist's shop or doctor's waiting room.

Sometimes a hiding place known as a 'drop' was used. This could be almost anywhere—a crack in a wall, a hollow log—as long as the pick-up could be made without suspicion. Networks also needed 'safe houses' (secure addresses where agents could go into hiding).

Bulky material such as maps and diagrams was often carried by hand to the intelligence base. (The French agent, Michel Hollard, crossed the Swiss border 98 times to reach Allied intelligence.)

Other material might be photographed, reduced to a microdot and sent through the post. But this method was slow. For swift, long-distance transmission, radio contact was best.

The Red Orchestra

The Russians had set up networks before war broke out. As soon as Germany invaded Russia, Nazi counter-espionage technicians began to notice that masses of coded information was being transmitted to Moscow from bases throughout western Europe.

The Germans nicknamed this network the Red Orchestra, and made breaking its rings a top priority.

The head of the Orchestra was a Polish Communist called Leopold Trepper, who travelled between his bases in Brussels, Amsterdam, Berlin, Marseilles and Paris under various false identities.

Trepper's work led him into many narrow scrapes. Once, he arrived at a radio operator's flat to find it crammed with German agents. The safe house had been blown. Trepper coolly persuaded the Germans that he was just a travelling salesman and escaped.

Several German opponents of Nazism played key roles in feeding intelligence to the Orchestra. It was one way of resisting Hitler.

The Red Orchestra had German agents inside Nazi ministries. Between 1940 and 1943, the network sent about 1500 dispatches to 'the Centre' in Moscow (the Russian intelligence base). But using radio direction-finders, code-breakers and double agents, the Nazis eventually penetrated the rings.

One after another, the captured agents were savagely tortured to reveal their accomplices. Over one hundred agents were eventually executed, died under torture or committed suicide in enemy hands.

Trepper himself was finally tracked down and arrested while at his dentist. The Germans tried to 'turn him round' (persuade him to work for them) and send misleading information to Moscow.

Trepper pretended to play along for a while, but really warned Moscow of what was going on. Then he escaped again.

Above: **A 'safe house' was a safe address used by a network. Flats in large apartment blocks were hard for the enemy to keep under surveillance.**

Above: **A 'cut-out' protected the identity of the network's director, so that, ideally, neither the enemy nor his own spies knew who he was.**

Above: **A 'drop' or 'dead letter box' was a safe hiding place for messages which could be left there, and picked up later by an agent's contact.**

Right: **The key figures in the Lucy Ring.
Who was Lucy's source? It is now suggested
that Lucy worked for the British. His
information was Ultra material (see page 29)
which the British wanted to give to Russia
without revealing its origin.**

**The ring used three radio transmitters.
'Jim' was an Englishman called Alexander
Foote. He had been recruited as a Communist
spy before the war, but it is possible that he
too was working for the British all along.**

The Lucy Ring

Trepper's organization was broken. But
another Russian ring was still operating
from Switzerland. This neutral state in
the heart of Nazi Europe was a hive of
intelligence activity.

The ring was run by a Hungarian Com-
munist called Sandor Rado ('Dora').
Three transmitters bombarded the
Centre with top-level intelligence about
German troop movements, armaments
and strategy in Russia.

The best information came from a man
called Rudolf Roessler (code-named
'Lucy' because he worked in Lucerne).
He seemed to have had contacts at the
highest levels in the German army because his reports were amazingly detailed and up-to-date.

Lucy's reports affected the outcome of
the Battle of Kursk in July 1943. He sent
advance information about the German
plans of attack, allowing the Russians
to prepare for the onslaught with
trenches and minefields. In a colossal
tank battle, the Germans were halted.

The 'Lucy Ring' was eventually broken
up by Swiss police acting under pressure
from the Germans. But it had already
contributed to Russia's crucial victories.

Above: **'Lucy' (Rudolf Roessler)** was a
German exile. He worked for Swiss military
intelligence, but mystery still surrounds his
top level sources, supposedly inside Nazi
Germany. Roessler died in 1958.

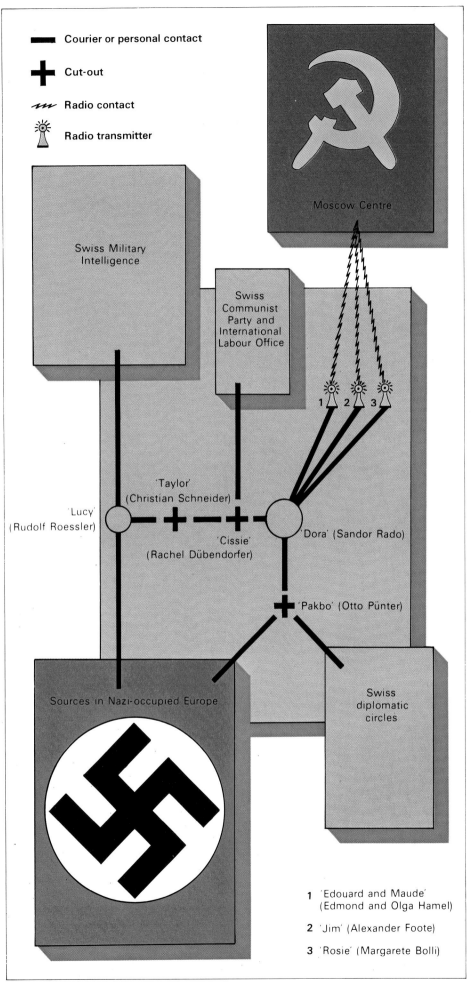

Courier or personal contact

Cut-out

Radio contact

Radio transmitter

Moscow Centre

Swiss Military
Intelligence

Swiss
Communist
Party and
International
Labour Office

1 2 3

'Taylor'
(Christian Schneider)

'Lucy'
(Rudolf Roessler)

'Cissie'
(Rachel Dübendorfer)

'Dora' (Sandor Rado)

'Pakbo' (Otto Pünter)

Sources in Nazi-occupied Europe

Swiss
diplomatic
circles

1 'Edouard and Maude'
(Edmond and Olga Hamel)

2 'Jim' (Alexander Foote)

3 'Rosie' (Margarete Bolli)

SPECIAL OPERATIONS

Subversion

The Allies set up special agencies to encourage subversion in occupied Europe. They were intended to recruit and equip secret armies, providing tools and training for sabotage.

Subversion was kept largely separate from espionage. After all, saboteurs could rarely avoid attracting attention, while spies needed secrecy for their work. In fact, there were frequent arguments between the intelligence services and the subversion agencies.

Russian agents were trained by the NKVD. In Britain a body called the Special Operations Executive (SOE) trained both British agents, and exiles from the occupied countries.

The American OSS was partly modelled on SOE, and the two agencies worked closely together. OSS had its own training schools near Washington, but many American agents were trained at an SOE school near Toronto in Canada. Similarly, SOE agents were often dropped into Europe from American aircraft.

SOE training

Agents were recruited from every walk of life. They included former businessmen, teachers, secretaries and even two acrobats (the Newton brothers).

The headquarters of SOE were at 64 Baker Street, and there were several flats elsewhere in London where recruitment and briefing were carried out.

Agents began their training with a general aptitude test. Then they went on to a stiff commando course on the rocky west coast of Scotland. They learned armed and unarmed combat, methods of silent killing, weapons training and raiding tactics. They were taught how to demolish railways, read maps and signal in Morse code.

The next stage involved parachute training at Ringway near Manchester.

Left: **In 1944, the RAF made a film called 'Now It Can Be Told' (later re-named 'School for Danger'). The film was publicly released and describes the activities of the Special Operations Executive. Real agents took the leading roles: SOE's Harry Rée and Jacqueline Nearne.**

These pictures show them going through some of SOE's training courses.

1 Sabotage	**5 Tradecraft**
2 Physical training	**6 Parachute training**
3 Weapons	**7 Radio transmission**
4 Raiding tactics	

Below: **Weapons for silent killing:**
1 SOE Welrod silent pistol.
2 American OSS high standard H-D silent pistol.
3 SOE high standard Model 'B' silent pistol with magazine.
4 Fairburn and Sykes fighting knife.

The single-shot Welrod was a particularly useful weapon for the undercover agent. The butt could be detached from the barrel for concealment; the pistol could be hidden in a trouser-leg. It was devised by SOE's experimental station near Welwyn, which also produced the Welman midget submarine.

Undercover work

Next, agents were sent to various country houses in the New Forest where they learned about undercover work.

They were taught how to memorize a cover story, arrange a rendezvous (secret meeting) and establish contact by password. They faced tough mock interrogations, learned how to pick locks and break safes. The SOE heroine, Violette Szabo, joked that she had been equipped for a wonderful career after the war—as a cat burglar.

There was practice in how to spot and lose a 'tail'. One agent, the novelist John Lodwick, has described trips to Bournemouth where agents would play 'games of follow-my-leader through Woolworth's and the second-class hotels'.

Besides such general courses, there were specialist schools for radio operators and saboteurs. Dummy vessels were blown up on the Manchester Ship Canal.

As in all schools, there were pupils who gave little attention to their instructors. Some paid the penalty later. But although the course was not perfect, the agents had gained much dangerous knowledge. Those who proved untrustworthy were sent to workshops in the Scottish Highlands, where they remained until it was safe to release them.

Those who passed were sent to holding schools near the airfields from which they were to take off on their missions.

Final touches

SOE had its own tailor's workshop which produced clothing for Europe (for example, Parisian women wore their jackets at least 25 centimetres longer than English women).

Foreign labels were stitched into the linings, and clothes had to be worn in as well so as not to look too new. Before take-off, pockets were searched for any material, such as an English theatre ticket stub, which might give the agent away in Europe.

Both SOE and OSS had departments which produced forged papers. Cunning gadgets were also designed for secret operations. SOE weapons included the single-shot Welrod silent pistol and a gas gun disguised as a fountain pen.

Finally, agents were issued with lethal cyanide capsules (L pills). Gestapo methods were well known, and suicide might be preferable to interrogation.

NIGHT LANDINGS

Pilot's cockpit

Bristol *Mercury*
890-hp engine

Bomb housings removed

By sea and air

Getting agents in and out of occupied Europe was a dangerous business. Some agents went by submarine or motor torpedo boat, arriving silently at dead of night. But such operations were rare. Submarines especially were seldom available for secret operations.

Other agents travelled hidden in local vessels: trawlers in the North Sea, feluccas in the Mediterranean and caiques in the Aegean. But enemy coastal patrols made this risky and it was always slow. Landing from the air was swifter.

A great many agents dropped by parachute. They went at night, wearing civilian clothes under parachute suits, and equipped with their forged papers, money, weapons, benzedrine tablets and L pill.

Many of the first agents dropped 'blind'; they had no-one waiting for them when they landed. They carried spades, for burying the parachute was vitally important.

Later in the war, reception committees of resistance workers might be ready on the ground, with a pit already dug for the parachute.

Parachuting was dangerous. Several agents were killed, or badly injured, on landing. Equipment might be smashed or lost. Besides, parachutes did not offer a way *out* of Europe, so aircraft were also used to make landings.

A few large American Hudsons and Dakotas were used towards the end of the war. But generally, the little British Lysander proved the most suitable plane for this work.

Right: **SOE's Jacqueline Nearne in parachute kit. Agents wore padded overalls, with helmets and spine pads to give some protection on landing.**

Maps, compasses, knives and pistols were carried in the zipper pockets. Heavier equipment, such as radio transmitters and explosives, was dropped on separate parachutes, packed in sponge rubber and heavy canvas.

The night-time drops were normally made too low over the ground to allow parachutists to operate their own ripcords. So-called 'static lines', attached to the plane, tugged the parachutes open as the agents went through the hole.

Jacqueline Nearne was dropped into France in January 1943. Her English companion, Maurice Southgate, made an awful blunder soon after the landing. He asked the first peasant he met when the next bus passed—in English!

But both survived the slip-up. Nearne acted as a courier, maintaining contact between different SOE 'circuits' in a wide area stretching far to the south and west of Paris.

She was brought out by Lysander in April 1944, and awarded the MBE for her valuable work.

Lysander flights

The 'Lizzie' was easy to manoeuvre, avoiding German flak at the coast. It could fly at low speeds over hedgerows and only needed a firm, flat field about 600 metres square to land in.

However, flights had to be made during the 'moon period'. This was a few nights each month when the moon was full enough to provide light for navigation. Even then, bad weather, fog, or failure to find the landing field caused many missions to be abandoned.

Landing drill was carefully worked out. A reception committee laid out a simple flight path with three pocket torches or bicycle lamps. A fourth light was used to flash a pre-arranged Morse letter. The pilot was not supposed to land unless the right letter was flashed.

Below: **The Westland Lysander had been designed as a lightly armed army cooperation aircraft. Its steel, V-shaped wing supports made it very sturdy. But it had to be adapted slightly for secret operations.**

Its small bomb housings were removed. The gun emplacement was taken out to leave space for three (or, at a squeeze, four) agents.

A steel ladder was added at the side to make getting in and out easier. An extra **fuel tank gave a longer range and allowed flights deep into France.**

The first models were painted black all over for night-time camouflage. But it was found that they stood out too well when seen from above by enemy fighters. The upper surfaces were then painted green and grey as camouflage against the ground. The lower surfaces remained black so that it was very hard to detect the plane against the night sky.

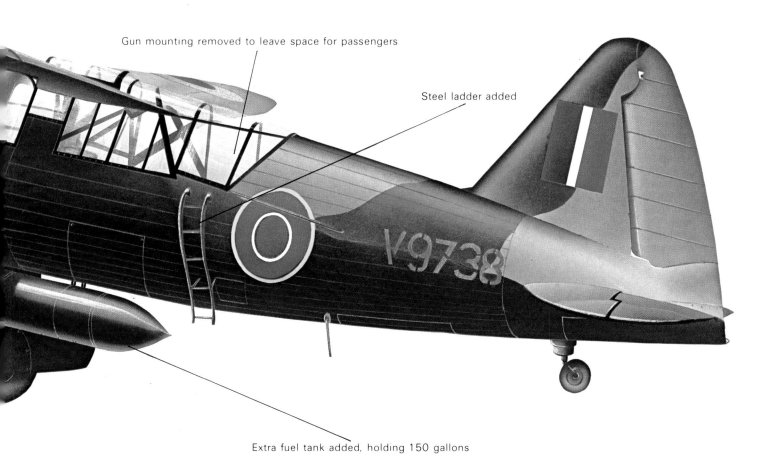

Gun mounting removed to leave space for passengers

Steel ladder added

Extra fuel tank added, holding 150 gallons

Sometimes the reception committee also used a short-wave radio known as an S-phone to guide the pilot down. In the later part of the war, a radar device called Eureka also became available.

The agents were known as 'Joes' to the pilots. After a successful landing they would climb out of the plane and a new batch, bound for England would climb in. As a mark of thanks, the reception committee sometimes gave gifts of perfume and champagne to the pilot before he took off again.

Of course, landings did not always go smoothly. There were many dramas, particularly when muddy fields or damage on landing made it hard to take off again. Once, half a French village and a team of carthorses were needed to pull a Hudson free from a soft landing ground.

Dangers

One pilot, Flight Commander 'Sticky' Murphy, met a German ambush on landing. He wheeled round and took off as the firing started. Bullets smashed into the plane and he was shot through the neck. Bleeding and giddy, he managed to reach home. On arrival, 30 German bullets were found in the aircraft.

There were other dangers. One French organizer of reception committees was tipping the Germans off about the landings. Some agents were tailed on arrival to discover their destinations.

But in general, the moon landings were a great success. At least 180 Lysander flights were made to France alone. Only thirteen planes were lost and six pilots killed; a good record by wartime standards.

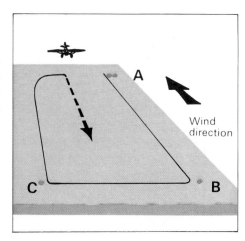

Above: **Landing drill. The reception committee laid out an L-shaped arrangement of lights. The pilot touched down at A, taxied round B and C before returning to halt at A. (The second light at A flashed the Morse landing signal.)**

UNDERGROUND ARMIES

Scattered units

At the beginning of the Occupation, a few patriots had gone into hiding, anxious to take positive action against the Germans. When the enemy imposed compulsory labour service, thousands more fled their homes. They were forced to live like outlaws and provided useful recruits for the Resistance.

Some built makeshift camps in forests or mountains. The French term for these outlaw groups was *maquis* (a Corsican bandit word meaning brushland).

Others helped them by keeping up their normal lives and working under-cover. This was particularly necessary in countries like Denmark and Holland with few remote regions.

Gradually, the scattered units began to form undercover armies. Some had proper ranks and even some sort of uniform. They established links with their governments-in-exile and in some cases took direct orders from them: like the Home Army in Poland, Norway's Milorg and the Belgian Secret Army.

But others remained independent. The Communists in particular tended to keep themselves to themselves. Uniting the rival groups was a problem. Each suspected the other of wanting to seize power after the war.

At first, it was hoped that underground groups could wage a permanent guerilla war against the Germans. In Churchill's words, they might 'set Europe ablaze'. But it soon became clear that the scattered units were no match for Germany's modern war machine.

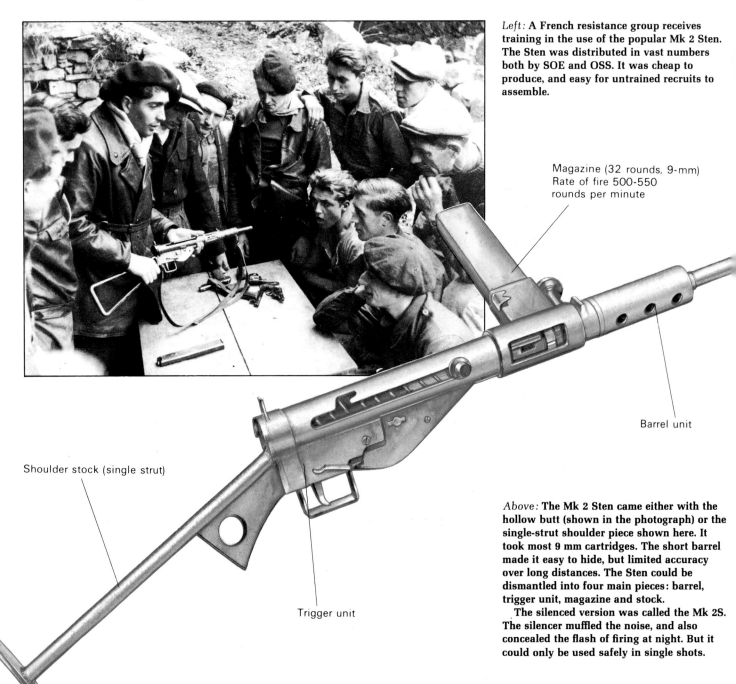

Left: **A French resistance group receives training in the use of the popular Mk 2 Sten. The Sten was distributed in vast numbers both by SOE and OSS. It was cheap to produce, and easy for untrained recruits to assemble.**

Magazine (32 rounds, 9-mm)
Rate of fire 500-550 rounds per minute

Barrel unit

Shoulder stock (single strut)

Trigger unit

Above: **The Mk 2 Sten came either with the hollow butt (shown in the photograph) or the single-strut shoulder piece shown here. It took most 9 mm cartridges. The short barrel made it easy to hide, but limited accuracy over long distances. The Sten could be dismantled into four main pieces: barrel, trigger unit, magazine and stock.**

The silenced version was called the Mk 2S. The silencer muffled the noise, and also concealed the flash of firing at night. But it could only be used safely in single shots.

Flash absorber (to hide flash of firing at night)

Magazine (30 rounds, .303) Rate of fire 500 rounds per minute

Magazine catch

Fore sight

Hand-grip

Back sight

Rifled barrel

Piston

Gas cylinder

Breech block and loading mechanism

Above: **The Bren was a light machine gun. It was generally fired from its forked support from a hidden position. For this reason, it was more useful to rural units than to groups operating in towns.**

Above: **In 1939 Jean Moulin ('Rex' or 'Max') was the French prefect of Chartres. The Germans tried to make him blame certain atrocities on the wrong people. Rather than agree, he tried to cut his throat (afterwards he always wore a scarf to hide the scars). Moulin was later responsible for unifying the different French resistance movements under de Gaulle's leadership in a National Resistance Council (CNR). Captured in 1943, he was terribly tortured and died in German hands. He gave nothing away.**

Aims and equipment

SOE and OSS advised the secret armies of Western Europe to lie low. They should engage in sabotage, gather recruits, build up arms and supplies, receive training and co-ordinate.

Then, when the invasion of Europe was launched, they should rise in revolt to cause havoc behind German lines.

There was much to be done. Weapons and explosives were smuggled into Europe by sea routes, or dropped by parachute in canisters.

Landing fields had to be found for the supply drops, and farm carts brought in to remove heavy equipment.

Safe houses had to be found for incoming agents and hiding places were needed for arms dumps. Some wise resisters kept two arms dumps, one large and one small. If a member was tortured he need only reveal the smaller one.

The secret armies were best suited for hit-and-run actions. The most useful weapons were those that could be used at close range: grenades, pistols, rifles and sub-machine-guns.

The Mk 2 Sten was a particular favourite. It was light, easy to use and easy to hide. The dismantled parts could be carried in a large handbag.

It could also be fitted with a silencer for secret operations. But it did have its faults. It was not very accurate at a distance, and it had a tendency to jam.

Bazookas and light machine-guns, such as the Bren, were also supplied. Ambitious groups often wanted heavier equipment still, but it was rarely supplied until the end of the war.

Not all the underground groups were in contact with the Allies, so they had to find their own weapons. Stealing from the Germans was common. Young resisters would lift revolvers from their holsters in restaurant cloakrooms, or rifles from railway platforms.

Captured German Luger pistols and 'Schmeisser' sub-machine-guns became prized weapons of the Resistance. And if all else failed, a carving knife or pitchfork could be deadly.

In town and country

Urban groups lived like hunted gangsters. They provided small teams of gunmen as protection squads for saboteurs. They organized raids on German supply dumps, and supervized the liquidation of informers. Inevitably, the violence attracted some shady characters.

But anyone might take up arms. Lucie Aubrac took part in a raid to rescue her husband from a Gestapo lorry in Lyons. It was a brilliant success—and she was six months' pregnant at the time.

Rural groups rarely numbered more than 20 or 30 people. The Gaullists did build up units of several hundred in some remote regions, but these were unwieldy.

Food, warm clothing and medical supplies were vital to rural groups. With the scarcity of petrol, bicycles were widely used. Good walking boots were essential.

One maquis member, who had been captured and tortured by the Gestapo, managed to escape from his cell in his stockinged feet. Then he remembered his boots, tiptoed back past sleeping sentries to collect them; and escaped again.

PARTISANS

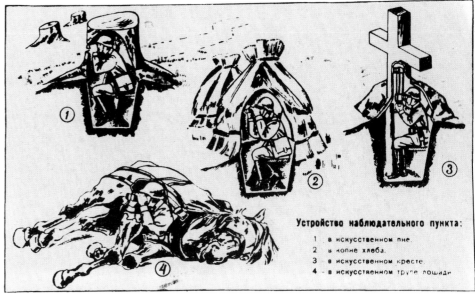

Above: **This picture from a Red Army handbook shows four different ways of** hiding an observation post. The partisans developed similar skills in camouflage.

Freedom fighters

Southern and Eastern Europe included vast expanses of forests, swamps and mountains where armies of freedom fighters, known as partisans, sprang up. Here it was possible to wage permanent guerilla war against the enemy, and so the Allies encouraged it.

One aim was to pin down vital German units which might otherwise be used elsewhere. Another was to disrupt the German supply lines which ran south to North Africa and the Near East.

Partisans were active in Russia, Yugoslavia, Greece and Albania. When the Allies invaded Fascist Italy in 1943, many Italians also took to the hills to fight in partisan armies alongside the Allies.

Russia was never wholly occupied by the Germans, and the partisans acted as a fighting wing of the regular army, crossing the long fighting front by remote forest paths.

Courier planes sometimes carried messages to and fro, while NKVD instruction teams gave training in sabotage and assassination. A handbook for partisans was printed, describing everything from how to demolish a railway to recipes for hedgehog stew.

Partisan life

Partisan life was broadly the same everywhere. The freedom fighters had to travel light, hit hard and run fast. They had to keep on good terms with the local people, for they relied on them for food and shelter.

The enemy granted no mercy. Captive partisans were shot—or worse. (Once, the Germans finished off scores of wounded Yugoslav partisans by driving tanks over them.)

Protecting the wounded was a problem for the fast-moving guerillas. When possible, they took their sick with them.

They were often desperately short of medical supplies. Sometimes, bandages were even taken from the dying, rinsed in streams and used on the living.

Above: **Russian partisans go into action in the Ukraine. Small, hard hitting groups** struck at the enemy wherever, and whenever, they were least expected.

Above: **Russian partisans make their way along a hidden trail. They are carrying a** wounded comrade with them, rather than leaving him to certain death in enemy hands.

22

Living rough

The partisans developed specialist skills in camouflage. They set up hidden hospitals in caves, forest shelters, or even dug them underground.

In Yugoslavia, approaches to the hospitals were blocked by barriers of logs and brushwood. All footprints were swept away daily and covered with snow in winter.

Sentries mounted guard over partisan camps, surveying the surrounding area from hidden observation posts. The camps themselves had to be invisible from above, for the enemy used aircraft against the partisans. Greek guerillas built shelters like wigwams from branches of fir trees.

Partisans often went hungry, especially in winter. They were sometimes reduced to eating clover and brewing soup from nettles.

A savage war

Partisan warfare was waged with great savagery on both sides, and German reprisals against local people were exceptionally fierce. At Kragujevac in Yugoslavia, 5000 male hostages were shot in one day after a skirmish with partisans nearby.

Villages were burnt on the slightest suspicion of partisan sympathies, and their populations forced into hiding. Once, 90 Yugoslav villagers hid in a cave while a German patrol passed. A baby started crying. The mother strangled it rather than let it betray their position.

The horrors of partisan warfare were multiplied in Greece and Yugoslavia. Both held rival partisan armies: Communist and non-Communist. In both countries, the partisans fought each other as well as the enemy.

The western Allies supported the non-Communists in Greece. But in Yugoslavia, they found that some non-Communist units were collaborating openly with the Germans and their Italian allies.

Gradually, the western Allies began to switch their support to the Communist partisans, headed by Josip Broz (code-named 'Tito').

Tito showed a real flair for guerilla warfare. He received no help from Britain or America until mid-1943, and none from Russia until 1944. Yet his armies held whole regions for long periods against overwhelmingly superior enemy forces. Vital German resources were diverted to meet the partisan challenge.

Above: **Captured German weapons were widely used by the partisans:**
1 **German KAW-98K rifle.**
2 **MP-40 'Schmeisser' sub-machine-gun.**
3 **Walther P-38 automatic pistol.**
4 **Standard hand-grenade.**

Right: **A girl partisan in Tito's army, where women sometimes fought beside the men. The partisans wore whatever came to hand. The only true 'uniform' was the red star cap badge. This girl carries a 'Schmeisser'.**

Above: **Tito dictates marching orders from a forest hideaway. Strips of Yugoslavia were parcelled out among Germany's satellites. Besides foreign enemies, the Communist partisans were fighting a civil war with nationalist partisans and collaborators.**

SABOTAGE

Above: **French saboteurs laying charges on a length of track (1944). The wadges of plastic explosive could be fixed to a rail by smearing them with Vaseline. The charges are linked with safety fuse.**

Left: **Teenage members of the Danish Resistance travelling to a sabotage operation in a sealed van. They are armed with Stens and will keep look-out while the saboteurs get down to business.**

Disruption

Sabotage was one of the main roles of the Resistance. It involved hindering the production of enemy supplies, disrupting communications and damaging the German war effort in every possible way.

Some methods had simple nuisance value. People involved in war work for the Germans could do their jobs slowly or badly. Some industries could be disrupted by breaking, or removing, an important machine part.

A handful of iron filings could ruin a piece of delicate machinery. SOE produced a grease which destroyed the parts it was supposed to lubricate.

The smallest opportunities were snatched to make life uncomfortable for the enemy. Once, a batch of shirts bound for a German U-boat station was treated with itching powder by resistance workers in the factory.

Railwaymen were among the most dedicated resisters. Sometimes, whole truckloads of supplies simply 'disappeared'. Another trick was to switch the labels on sealed trucks bound for different places.

For example, a German airfield expecting machine parts was once sent a consignment of rotten fruit.

The great advantage of this ploy was that the 'mistake' seemed accidental, and it was hard to trace who was responsible. All the same, several railwaymen were shot for such actions.

Obviously, much damage could be done with explosives. The Allied agencies supplied trained agents, equipment, advice and instruction leaflets.

Bridges and railways

In 1942, SOE instructors and Greek partisans cooperated in a dramatically successful operation. They blew up the Gorgopotamos viaduct, which carried the only railway line between southern Greece and Nazi Europe.

The biggest bangs did not necessarily do the greatest damage. Saboteurs were taught to recognize the most vulnerable part of a machine, and to strike at the items which were hardest to replace.

In his book, *Maquis*, SOE's George Millar describes how his small resistance group put the great turntables at Besançon station out of action with modest charges on the two central pivots.

As a result, 63 big locomotives needed by the Germans were imprisoned for weeks in their roundhouses.

Plastic explosive

Home-made bombs could be put together from everyday materials, and saboteurs also used dynamite and gelignite. But a new invention called plastic explosive was more adaptable.

Plastic explosive consisted of cyclonite mixed with a substance which allowed it to be moulded like putty. It could be fixed to an object with adhesive tape. Cased in metal and with magnets attached, it could also be used underwater as a limpet mine.

'Plastic' was safe to carry around, and would even burn without exploding. It needed a detonation to set it off. Small priming charges were pressed in to provide the detonation, with time fuses to give the saboteur time to get away.

SOE supplied pencil-shaped fuses which were colour coded according to the delay needed. But even a household alarm clock could be rigged up as a delayed action device.

Better than bombs

Saboteurs could sometimes reach targets which aircraft could not. The wolfram mines of central France were an example.

Wolfram was a vital ore needed for making armoured plate and armour-piercing ammunition. The French mines were the only ones inside occupied Europe, but they were too small and well hidden for Allied bombers to tackle.

In three raids, resisters put the mines out of action. Then the Germans sent in soldiers to man the main mine. But on 14 July 1944, the Resistance captured it and held it until the Liberation.

Sabotage had another advantage over aerial bombardment. It could avoid heavy civilian casualties.

The Peugeot car factory in Mont-béliard in eastern France had been taken over to make gun carriers and tank tracks for the German army. The RAF made one failed attempt to bomb the works; many townspeople were killed.

SOE's Harry Rée was already in friendly contact with Rodolph Peugeot (a director of the firm), who agreed to let the factory be sabotaged from within. The RAF agreed to keep away if regular sabotage could be kept up.

Rée set up a team at the factory, and their sabotage operations lasted until the town was liberated. The RAF never returned.

Below: **Sabotaging trains carrying goods for Germany was a frequent activity. Railway workers sometimes helped by guiding a 'runaway' train along the track to pile into the wreckage.**

THE RADIO WAR

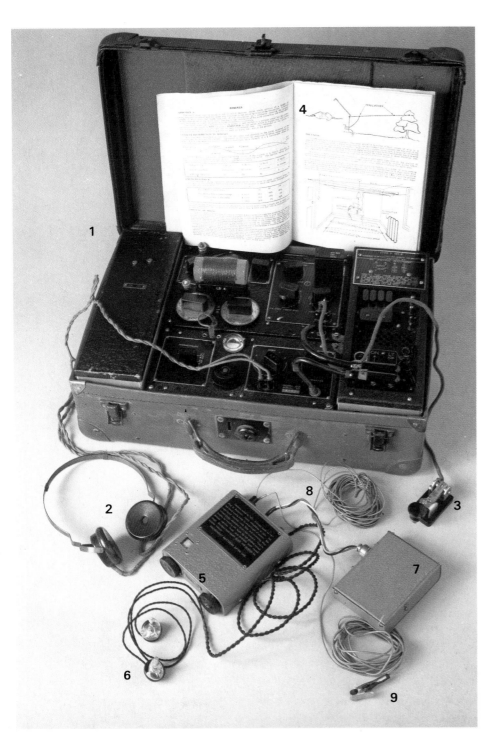

Above: **SOE equipment for secret radio:**
Type 3 Mk II transceiver (1), with headphones (2), Morse key (3) and instruction manual (4).
Sets this size were dangerous to carry around in public. There was always the danger of a snap check or train inspection.

The Type 31-1 pocket receiver (5) came later in the war. It is shown here with its earphones (6), battery pack (7), aerial (8) and earth (9).
This compact device could only receive messages; it did not transmit them. Pocket transmitters were also developed.

Radio contact

Contact with a resistance group's base abroad was vital. During the early months of the war, carrier pigeons were still used to send long-distance messages, as they had been in World War One. But secret radio transmission soon replaced them.

The most commonly used sets were about the size of a small suitcase (though more compact ones were developed as the war went on). Technically, they were known as 'transceivers', that is, sets which could both transmit and receive messages.

The messages themselves were sent in cipher and tapped out in Morse code (the human voice was never used).

The operators, sometimes known as 'pianists', often lived in permanent hiding. Their lives were organized around pre-arranged times for transmission to London or Moscow.

Many SOE operators were women. Among them was an Indian princess, Noor Inayat Khan ('Madeleine'). She was later arrested, and shot at Dachau in 1944.

Detectors

The Germans had an efficient system for locating transmitters. There were permanent direction-finding stations positioned around Europe to identify the area from which messages were being sent.

Once a town had been located, mobile teams of detector vans (sometimes disguised as ambulances) would cruise slowly through the streets to get a more exact bearing.

Finally, agents on foot might be needed to circle the area and pinpoint the building itself. They wore their hats pulled down and collars up to hide their headphones, and muttered into their walkie-talkies.

Wise operators had a permanent lookout in position during transmission. Ideally, the pianist would operate from an attic room overlooking other buildings to allow clear reception. Isolated farmhouses were also used, though they were easier targets for enemy direction-finders.

Messages had to be short and sharp. It was said that the Germans could pinpoint a transmitter within 20 minutes of receiving a signal. Every second spent at the set might be bringing the detectors closer.

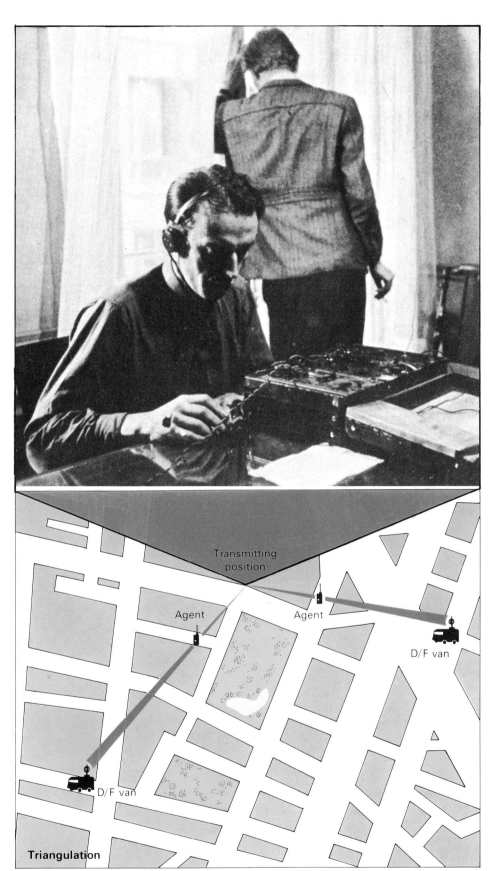

Triangulation

Precautions

If possible, operators would change their transmitting positions from time to time. Some built secret compartments to hide their equipment in daytime, or dismantled it when off the air. But they were often tempted to relax their security.

Alexander Foote, who worked with the Lucy Ring, described the sheer nuisance of taking constant precautions:

'For anyone who wishes to indulge in espionage I do not recommend digging in a flower-bed for a biscuit tin containing the essential parts of a transmitter with the scheduled time for transmission fast approaching.'

The radio operator was the key agent in any network, and the capture of a transmitter could be disastrous. It broke the vital link with the base abroad. If the enemy also cracked the operator's cipher, he could use it to send back false information. The Germans called this method of deception the *Funkspiel* (radio game).

Operation North Pole

One disastrous example, Operation North Pole, occurred in Holland. In March 1942, the German Abwehr colonel, H. J. Giskes, captured an SOE transmitter with its operator. He forced the man to send messages, claiming ambitious plans for the Dutch Resistance.

More and more agents and equipment were requested. By May 1943, 52 agents and many tonnes of weapons, explosives, supplies and transmitters were dropped in. Of course, they were all immediately rounded up on arrival.

Most of the agents were executed. But two eventually managed to escape to Britain with news of what was going on.

There were ways of avoiding this kind of calamity. An operator's 'fist' (pattern of tapping out Morse) could be as distinctive as his or her handwriting. A stranger's hand at the key might be detected at home.

If operators were forced to transmit under threat of torture, they could alter their security check. This was a short code signal used to prove that they were operating freely.

In the North Pole disaster, several agents were forced to transmit, and some did alter their security checks to show they were under pressure. Incredibly, SOE did not seem to notice. Once, London even accused an operator of carelessness and reminded him to include his security check in future!

Above: **The photograph at the top shows a radio operator at work in France. His lookout is in position at the window.**

The Germans used a process known as 'triangulation' to locate a transmitter. Two (or more) of their vehicles would each chart the direction from which the signal was coming.

They could then find the position of the transmitter by plotting the point at which the signals crossed. In built-up areas, agents on foot might be needed to get an exact bearing.

Of course, the Germans could only take bearings while the operator was on the air, so messages had to be short.

CODES AND CIPHERS

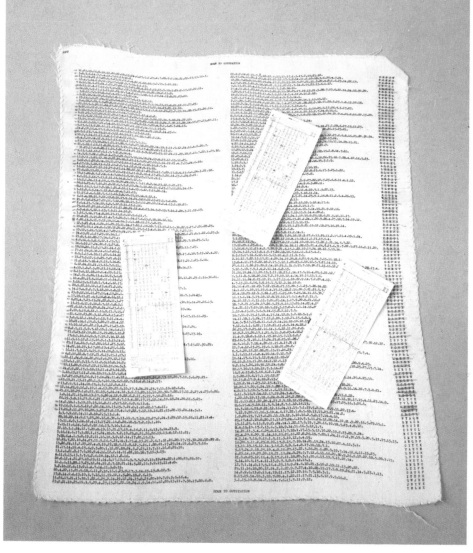

Codes

A code is a word or symbol that has a secret meaning. In the Lucy Ring, agents referred to the police as 'the doctor' and prison as 'hospital'. One day, Alexander Foote received this message over the phone:

'You will be sorry to hear that Edouard is much worse and the doctor has been called in. He decided after consultation that the only thing to do was to take him to hospital.'

Foote knew at once that Edmond Hamel had been arrested and imprisoned.

The BBC broadcast coded instructions to agents abroad at a certain hour every night: 'Barbara's dog will have three puppies', 'the dice are on the table', and similar phrases. The Germans could hear these strange announcements, of course. But the phrases were only understood by the agents concerned.

The broadcasts were particularly effective since a short code phrase could be used to give direct confirmation from London that an agent was trustworthy, or that an operation really did have official approval.

The agents themselves all had at least one code-name to protect their identity. De Gaulle's intelligence chiefs used the names of Paris underground stations: 'Passy', 'Rémy' and so on.

Some agents had different code-names for their different contacts. SOE's Yeo-Thomas was both 'Shelley' and 'the White Rabbit'.

Visual codes were also widely used. If the occupant of a safe house suspected that it was under surveillance, a flower pot could be placed in a particular window to warn other agents away.

Above: **A silk code sheet and signal plans used by an SOE radio operator, Yvonne Cormeau ('Annette'). She operated from a village in the foothills of the Pyrenees for over a year, and was never discovered by the Germans.**

Below: **A Belgian woman who worked in Ghent carried code messages for the Resistance, written on her back in invisible ink. She was discovered by the Germans and the photograph shows one of the messages revealed by a chemical developer.**

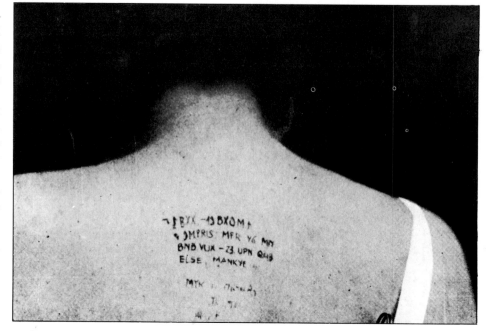

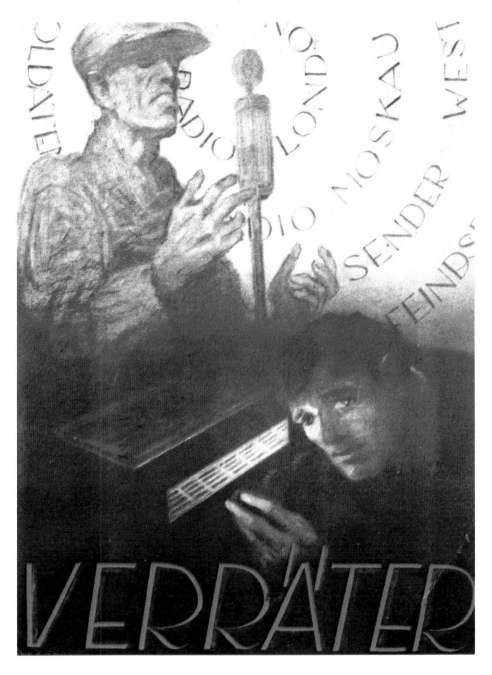

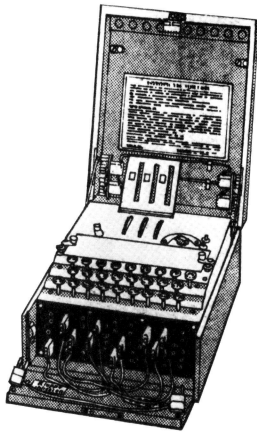

Above: **An early model of the German Enigma machine. It was shaped like a typewriter, with several revolving drums which produced enciphered letters at random. The Germans were constantly adapting and improving their Enigma system, and cracking it was an immense and complicated task.**

Ciphers

Only short, pre-arranged messages could be communicated in code. For longer reports, a cipher was needed.

A cipher is a way of re-arranging the whole alphabet using numbers, or switching letters. In its simplest form, each letter can be shifted one place along in the alphabet, so that CAT, for example, becomes DBU.

Some more secure systems involved using a key word or phrase known only to the sender and receiver. But given a fairly lengthy report, a cipher expert could still break the cipher.

The best cipher system was the One Time Pad. This was a booklet printed on silk for easy concealment. There were only two copies of each pad: one for the sender, one for the receiver. The cipher on each page was produced at random, used once, then destroyed.

Agents often kept some lighter fuel handy to burn their cipher in an emergency. This was vital for radio operators. The Germans kept records of all the radio traffic they overheard, even when they could not understand it. With the cipher in their hands, they could unravel all the earlier messages.

The Enigma machine

The Germans themselves used a battery-powered cipher machine called Enigma to transmit secret army commands, thinking the code unbreakable.

But even before war broke out, Polish and French intelligence had secretly co-operated to produce their own Enigma machines and smuggled one to Britain.

Deciphering Enigma messages during the war was a massive task. It was carried out at a top-secret cipher school at Bletchley in England.

Only a few people knew what was going on. The business of dealing with the mass of Enigma material on troop movements and strategic plans was given the code-name of Ultra. (The operation was only made public in 1972.)

Historians are still examining the impact of Ultra on the course of the war. But it now seems clear that advance knowledge of German intentions contributed greatly to some Allied victories; for example, in the Battle of Britain and Battle of the Atlantic.

Codes and ciphers were vital to secret communications. But there were dangers in trusting them too completely.

TRADECRAFT

Forgery and disguise

Well forged papers were vital, and might be needed in a hurry if an agent's cover had been blown. For good forgeries, expert skills were needed. Paper had to be exactly the right texture, and watermarks had to be faked.

Resistance groups sometimes used professional criminals for this work. They might also know a sympathetic policeman prepared to supply blank issues of genuine articles.

Despite precautions, SOE's forgers sometimes made mistakes. To distract inquisitive eyes, Yeo-Thomas used to carry a photograph of a naked girl in the celluloid window of his wallet.

If agents were pulled in for questioning, their papers would be checked against the records of the town which was supposed to have issed them. Forged cards were therefore often made out in the names of towns where the record office had been destroyed by bombing or sabotage.

Agents also needed to change their appearance. Elaborate wigs and make-up were rarely used. Simply putting on glasses and changing one's hairstyle were usually enough—and less easily spotted as disguise.

Hair dye might be needed. One Danish resister became famous for his flaming red hair which earned him the nickname of *Flammen*. In fact he had gained his trademark during a botched attempt to dye his blond hair brown.

Carrying messages

In resistance work there were always a lot of day-to-day arrangements to be made. Messages were passed back and forth, announcing the timing of a parachute drop, a new target for sabotage, the discovery of an informer and so on. Carrying bulky messages was a problem. SOE's Anne-Marie Walters wrote:

'Once, at a bus stop, I found myself in a snap control. One of the Germans searched my handbag while another examined my papers; he pulled out a crumpled little bunch of toilet paper and looked at me.

'I blushed modestly. He put it back tactfully. There were thirty BBC messages inside . . . I had blushed from sheer fright.'

Left: **A Danish forger at work for the Resistance.**

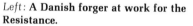
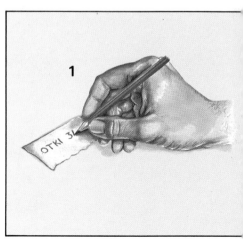

Security

Trained agents had a number of dos and don'ts drummed into them.

When they entered a building, they were to look for the exits in case they needed to make a quick getaway.

If a meeting took place in a bar or café, they should choose a corner seat giving them a good view of the street and the other customers.

When arranging a rendezvous, they were to inspect the area beforehand, arrive on time and leave at once if their contact had not turned up.

Yeo-Thomas was eventually caught by the enemy because he stayed too long at a rendezvous point. His contact had been arrested, and the Germans hurried to the spot where he was waiting.

The Germans often kept a suspect under surveillance for weeks if necessary in the hope of rounding up a whole network. So it was vital to keep alert at all times, even when there was no obvious reason to suspect danger.

Some big networks had an all-purpose password. It might be a question and answer, such as that used by the French 'Prosper' group: 'Where can I get lighter fuel?' 'Petrol, you mean?'

But if the Germans learnt the password they could infiltrate one of their own agents into the group.

There were other security checks. Agents who had not met before were sometimes each given half of a 100 franc note. If when they met they could fit the halves together, it was probably safe to exchange information.

Tradecraft did not guarantee safety, but it reduced risks. Some happy-go-lucky agents survived by sheer daring. But all too often, a careless agent quickly became a captured agent. And a captured agent brought suffering and death to his or her companions.

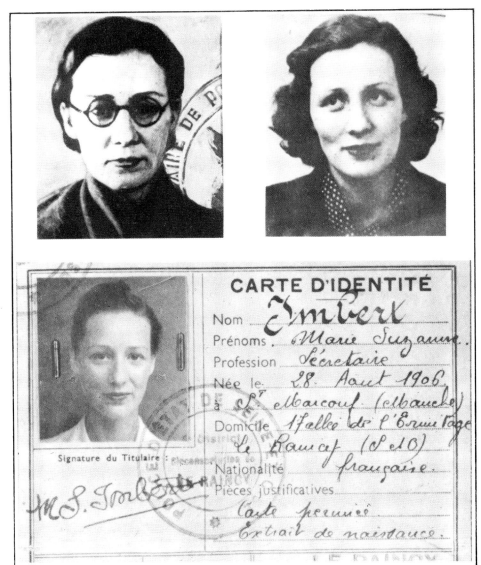

Above: **Three faces of Marie-Madeline Fourcade: as 'Madame Pezet, housewife' (top left); as 'Marie Suzanne Imbert, secretary' (bottom); from Gestapo records, (top right).**

Code-named 'Hedgehog', she came to head the huge French 'Alliance' network when its leader was arrested. 'Alliance' had about 3000 members, 500 of whom were killed. Agents used the code-names of animals, so the network was nicknamed 'Noah's Ark' by the Germans. Caught once, Fourcade escaped and continued her work.

Below: It was best for an agent not to carry any written messages at all; they could always lead to danger. But if a short message had to be put on paper, it could be written in code (1), rolled around a needle (2) and slipped into a cigarette (3). The needle was then withdrawn (4).

Concealed in this way, the message could be innocently passed to an agent's contact. It could also be smoked if an agent suspected that he or she was under surveillance by the enemy.

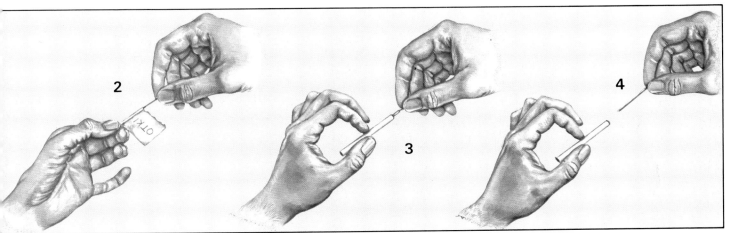

ESCAPE AND EVASION

Above: **How maps were smuggled in to prisoner-of-war camps in cards and games.**

The secret agencies

Throughout occupied Europe there were people on the run: workers avoiding labour service, Jewish refugees, escaped prisoners-of-war, fugitive agents and airmen who had been shot down.

Strictly speaking, they belonged to two types: escapers and evaders. Escapers were people who had already been captured (such as prisoners-of-war). Evaders were people who had never been in enemy hands (such as crashed airmen).

In Britain, a secret department called MI 9 was formed to encourage escape and evasion. The United States set up a similar body called MIS-X.

They provided tools and training, set up escape routes and gathered information from inside prisoner-of-war camps.

Escape aids

MI 9 and MIS-X kept in touch with prisoners through code messages in their personal mail. Escape aids were smuggled into camps in their parcels from home (the code messages explained where to find the equipment).

Maps were hidden in playing cards, forged passes were slipped inside chessboards. Tiny compasses were hidden in pipes and fountain pens. Capsules of dye for disguise were placed in tubes of toothpaste. MI 9 designed an all-purpose escaper's knife.

Bulkier items could sometimes be smuggled in by bribing the guards in the camp's parcels office. Radio receivers were even put together in a few camps.

MI 9 and MIS-X also briefed servicemen in evasion techniques in case they were stranded behind enemy lines. The Allies were desperately short of trained aircrew, and particular energy was devoted to helping them escape if they were shot down.

From 1940 onwards, all RAF pilots were equipped with a plastic box of evasion equipment (the same kit was issued to American aircrew from 1942).

It was designed to keep an airman alive for 48 hours after his crash.

A supply of foreign currency was included, with a passport photograph for forged papers. Maps were printed on fine silk so they would not rustle and compasses were hidden in tunic buttons.

Evasion techniques

Airmen were told that they must get clear of their wrecked plane. They then needed to get hold of workmen's clothes from sympathetic local people.

If they were walking to neutral territory they were told not to march in military fashion, but to slouch like tired labourers. They should pocket their wristwatches, for no workman would own one. Haversacks had to be slung over the shoulder, not carried on the back like a soldier's pack.

English evaders were not to use walking sticks, for Europeans rarely used them. When crossing a mountain frontier there was one vital rule of fieldcraft: never stand upright on the horizon.

Evaders were asked to keep their eyes open for anything of military importance. This might have intelligence value.

Lone evaders

Some evaders did make their way to freedom in this way. They slept rough in woods or hedgerows during the day, making long forced marches at night. (The Earl of Cardigan walked the length of France, from Boulogne into Spain.) Many received food, clothing and shelter from the ordinary people they met.

Evaders were warned of the dangers these civilians ran. The servicemen were unlikely to face more than the frustration of imprisonment if they were caught. But civilians risked their lives—and the lives of their families too.

In fact, however well disguised as a civilian an evader might be, he was advised to hold on to his service identity disc. It would be needed as proof of rank if he was captured. If he was thought to be a spy, or a resister, he could be shot.

Above: **Radio equipment in one camp was hidden in a gramophone.**

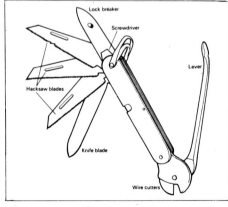

Above: **MI 9's all-purpose escaper's knife.**

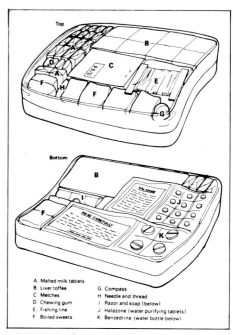

Above: **The evasion kit issued to airmen before they went out on their missions.**

A. Malted milk tablets
B. Liver toffee
C. Matches
D. Chewing gum
E. Fishing line
F. Boiled sweets
G. Compass
H. Needle and thread
I. Razor and soap (below)
J. Halazone (water purifying tablets)
K. Benzedrine (water bottle below)

Above: **Maps and compasses were hidden in airmen's buttons, lighters and shoe-heels.**

Above: **An RAF pilot in his flying kit. The fleece-lined flying boots were adapted for use in civilian disguise. When a taped section was removed from the ankles, the leg-pieces could be taken off to reveal underneath a pair of lace-up shoes.**

Right: **A lace in the black walking shoes held a flexible hacksaw blade. If the airman was captured by the enemy, this could be used to saw through the bars of his cell. The boots were cunningly devised, but airmen complained that they let in water.**

ESCAPE LINES

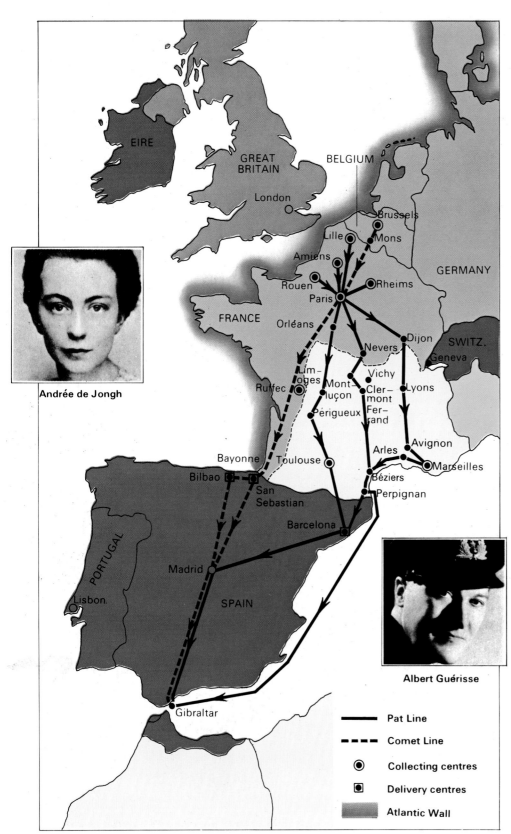

Andrée de Jongh

Albert Guérisse

Pat Line

Comet Line

Collecting centres

Delivery centres

Atlantic Wall

Finding a line

Many evaders were guided to freedom along escape lines run by the Resistance. These were chains of guides and safe houses running through occupied Europe and often beyond.

One way for an evader to find a line was to contact a country priest or the mother superior of a convent. Even if they were not involved in escape work themselves they often knew someone who was; and they would not betray a fugitive's trust.

The resistance workers kept watch for crashed planes and would try to find the crew before the Germans arrived.

Evaders would be hidden in barns or haystacks until the German search had been called off. An American airman called Mickey Coles fell right on to the roof of a farm building. The farmer quickly hid him in a cart, piled manure on top and stuck in a stove pipe so the airman could breathe.

The Germans searched the farm for nine hours. But Mickey Coles survived (though the smell of manure lingered about him for days).

Collecting centres

A fugitive would then be moved to a collecting centre. This was a safe house where evaders might be held for weeks before being moved on again.

Food, civilian clothes and forged papers were needed. Medical supplies hand to be on hand for the wounded.

Women played leading roles at the centres. Not all fugitives realized the dangers their hostesses were running. They often grew bored at the centres and might even slip out to explore the town.

There were worse dangers. The Germans often used agents posing as fugitives to try and penetrate the escape lines. So new arrivals would be thoroughly questioned to seek out spies. English airmen on one line were always asked 'What does Mrs Mopp say?'

Genuine RAF airmen were bound to know the answer: 'Can I do yer now, sir?' (Mrs Mopp was a charwoman in a popular British radio programme.)

Left: **Routes of the 'Comet' and 'Pat' lines, headed by Andrée de Jongh and Albert Guérisse. They ran south to Gibraltar to avoid the dangerous coastal zone along the Atlantic Wall. Some escapes were made by direct sea crossing from France to England, but the risks were great.**

Moving the fugitives

Once fugitives had been accepted on to a line they were issued with their forged papers and a change of clothing if necessary (for example, peasant clothes would attract attention in a big city). Pockets were scoured for items like English cigarettes which might give an airman away.

Guides then conducted batches of fugitives to the next centre. Some travelled on foot, by bicycle, or hidden in sealed trucks. Many made nerve-racking, silent, train journeys.

At times the tension of a train journey became almost unbearable. Once, the Belgian escape helper, Albert Guérisse, was escorting two airmen in the restaurant car of a train. One pilot accidentally spilled beer in the laps of two German soldiers.

The Germans rose, furiously mopping their trousers. In a fit of nerves the pilot suddenly burst into peals of uncontrollable laughter.

The terrified Guérisse began to apologize—then noticed that the Germans had started laughing too. Laughter is an international language and the whole carriage shook with guffaws. The crisis passed. But it could have led to death.

The Pat and Comet lines

Two of the best lines ran down through France, across the Pyrenees and into neutral Spain. The 'Comet' line was run by a 24-year-old Belgian girl called Andrée de Jongh. She received money from MI 9, but her helpers were all friends and acquaintances. Amazingly, this amateur network managed to guide over 700 evaders to freedom.

A similar number reached safety on Guérisse's 'Pat' line (so called because Guérisse used the cover name of 'Pat O'Leary'). He worked in closer contact with MI 9.

Local guides escorted fugitives across the Pyrenees by remote smugglers' paths. Even in Spain they were not safe, so the lines ran on to the tiny British colony of Gibraltar. Many fugitives crossed this last frontier in the boot of a car.

Both de Jongh and Guérisse were eventually betrayed to the Germans. Both ended up in concentration camps, but they both survived.

Escape work had real value. MI 9's lines alone are thought to have brought about 4000 airmen out of Europe—a great contribution to the Allied cause.

Above: **On rare occasions, important people were brought out of Europe by submarine. The Royal Navy's 'HMSM P-219' smuggled the escaped prisoner-of-war, General Giraud, from southern France to Gibraltar in 1942. (For a time, Giraud rivalled de Gaulle for leadership of the French Resistance.)**

Below: **An American pilot, Lieutenant Moore (kneeling, left), disguised as a peasant. Members of a French resistance group are showing him their store of weapons captured from the Germans. Airmen were told not to join in armed resistance themselves, but to get home as quickly as possible.**

CONCENTRATION CAMPS

Above: **Anne Frank. She wrote, 'This is a photo as I would wish myself to look all the time. Then I would maybe have a chance to come to Hollywood.'**
That chance never came. She was caught in hiding in 1944, and died in Belsen.

Right: **Some of the most notorious camps, with approximate figures for those who died in them. The centres specifically for mass extermination were built in occupied Poland. Hundreds of thousands also died in concentration camps on German soil.**

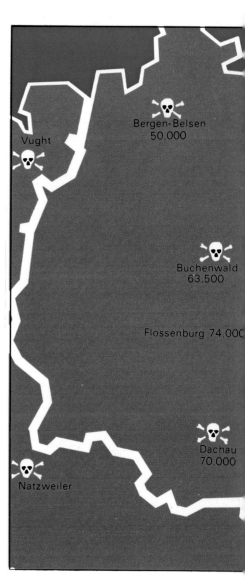

Bergen-Belsen
50,000

Vught

Buchenwald
63,500

Flossenburg 74,000

Dachau
70,000

Natzweiler

Above: **Jews from the Warsaw ghetto are rounded up during the doomed rising of 1943.**
The revolt began in January, when the SS tried to collect a new batch of prisoners for the camps. For months, the whole ghetto fought off massed German forces with rifles and home-made grenades. The Polish Home Army lent some assistance.
But the Germans sent in artillery to pound the rebels, and incendiaries to set the ghetto ablaze. In the end, the rising was crushed.

Persecution

The Nazis believed that they belonged to a superior race, and that Jews, Slavs, gypsies and others were inferior.

The persecution of Jews and other 'inferior' races began gradually in western Europe. Jews were made to wear the yellow Star of David on their clothes. They were forbidden to enter public places such as restaurants, cinemas, parks and even telephone booths. Everything was done to humiliate Jews and set them apart from other people.

Later, mass round-ups began. Whole families were herded on to trains bound for concentration camps.

Some Jews were kept hidden for years from the Nazis. In Holland, a schoolgirl called Anne Frank wrote a moving diary of her life in hiding.

The Danes managed to save almost all their Jewish population. Out of 7000, the Nazis were only able to round up about 800. The others had been smuggled to neutral Sweden (many German soldiers turned a blind eye to let them go).

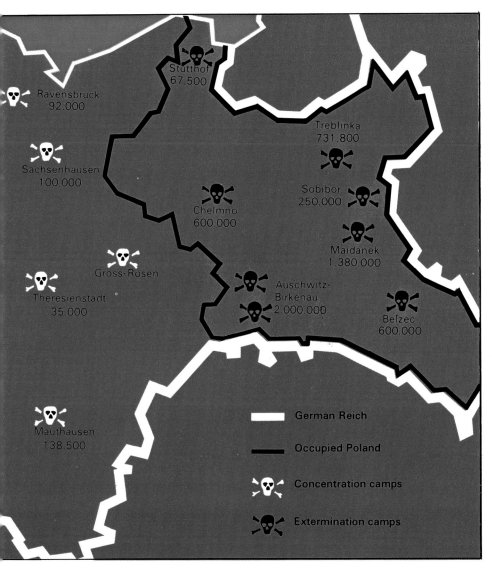

Ravensbruck
92,000

Stutthof
67,500

Treblinka
731,800

Sachsenhausen
100,000

Sobibor
250,000

Chelmno
600,000

Maidanek
1,380,000

Gross-Rosen

Theresienstadt
35,000

Auschwitz-
Birkenau
2,000,000

Belzec
600,000

Mauthausen
138,500

— German Reich

— Occupied Poland

Concentration camps

Extermination camps

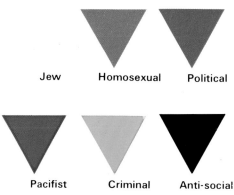

Jew   Homosexual   Political

Pacifist   Criminal   Anti-social

Above: **Prisoners in the camps were made to wear badges to denote their 'crime'.**

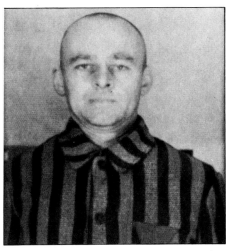

Above: **Witold Pilecki organized resistance in Auschwitz. In one escape, four prisoners got out disguised in SS uniform.**

Elsewhere, the proportion of escapes was far lower, and millions of men, women and children were rounded up.

Polish Jews were crammed into city areas known as ghettoes, and given barely enough food to survive. In 1943, the Warsaw ghetto rose in revolt. The rising was crushed. A handful of Jews escaped through the sewers, but nearly 80,000 died fighting or were sent to concentration camps.

Inside the camps

In the early days, no-one knew quite what awaited prisoners in the camps. In 1940, a member of the Polish Home Army, Witold Pilecki, volunteered to get himself sent to Auschwitz. For three years, he smuggled reports out.

Pilecki also formed resistance groups among the prisoners, to prepare for a possible rising. His reports were grim, including news of the gas chambers.

By 1942, it was clear that Auschwitz and certain other German camps in Poland had facilities for mass extermination. Men, women and children were being herded into the gas chambers, their bodies then burned in furnaces.

Even in camps not built for extermination, prisoners might be used as slave labour and worked until they dropped. Some were sent out to toil in mines and quarries.

Sadistic guards amused themselves by torturing and degrading their prisoners. Medical experiments were carried out on living people, without anaesthetic.

Terror was used as a deliberate policy to reduce the prisoners to a subhuman condition. The camps were surrounded by electric fences and minefields. Guards patrolled with whips and dogs.

For a single escape, hundreds of prisoners might be made to stand in the compound, naked and motionless for a whole winter's night. By the morning, many would have frozen to death.

The SS ran the camps for profit. Confiscated money, jewellery and other possessions were massed in warehouses. Gold fillings were picked from the teeth of the dead, and human hair was used to stuff pillows and mattresses.

Yet resistance did go on. At Sobibor, prisoners rushed the gates using makeshift weapons against their guards. About 400 got out, though most were killed beyond the gates.

Not all the prisoners were victims of racial persecution. Many political enemies and resistance workers ended up in the camps.

In a few cases, trained agents managed to survive while those around them failed. In fact, Pilecki escaped from Auschwitz, and SOE's Yeo-Thomas and Harry Peulevé escaped from Buchenwald. But these were rare exceptions.

Many other agents were shot during the last months of the war to prevent them from revealing the suffering they had endured in Nazi hands.

The sheer scale of the holocaust is hard to imagine. About six million people died in the camps. And the survivors were often scarred for life by the memories of what they had been through.

TARGET: SECRET WEAPONS

Above: **The Norsk Hydro plant in Norway. Here the Germans made heavy water for experiments with the atomic bomb. (The saboteurs' route is arrowed.)**

Below: **The last stocks of heavy water were carried by ferry. Haukelid placed his charges near the prow, so the vessel would sink nose first into the lake.**

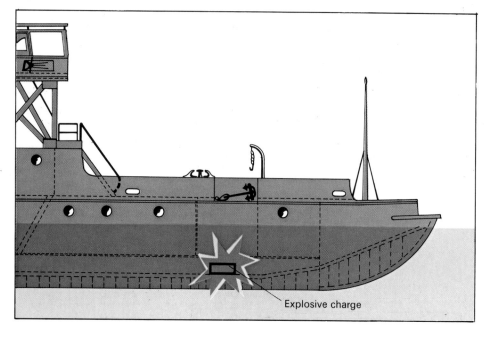

Explosive charge

Norsk Hydro

When the Germans occupied Norway, they seized the world's only heavy water plant. This was the Norsk Hydro works at Vermork. The heavy water was needed in some early experiments to make the atomic bomb.

Norsk Hydro was perched on a rocky slope among the forested mountains of southern Norway. Bombers could not be sure of hitting the target, so the Allies decided to mount a commando raid, using two gliders to land their men. Unluckily, both gliders crashed.

SOE took over. A scale model of the plant was built, and six Norwegian soldiers were trained on dummy targets. The team was code-named 'Gunnerside' and in February 1943 it was dropped in a remote region far from Vemork.

First they made contact with a three-man advance group (code-named 'Swallow') which had been waiting in place since before the failed commando raid. Together, they ski-trekked to Vemork, wearing white camouflage suits.

Eventually, they found a way up to the plant, cut their way into the compound and placed their charges. They had just got out when the explosives went off.

The operation was perfect. The heavy water tanks were destroyed—and no lives had been lost.

The two teams raced to Sweden, leaving Knut Haukelid from 'Gunnerside' behind with a radio operator from 'Swallow'.

After some months, the Germans began stockpiling heavy water again. Norsk Hydro was now too well guarded for a second sabotage operation, so the Allies had to use bombers.

On 16 November 1943, a mass flight of B-17 Flying Fortresses rained bombs on to the site. Norsk Hydro was wrecked but the last stocks of heavy water remained intact in concrete bunkers.

The Nazis now decided to move these last supplies to Germany. But Haukelid discovered the route. He and a team of resisters managed to place explosives in the bows of a ferry which was to take the heavy water across a lake. The charges were set to go off as the boat reached the deepest spot.

They went off right on time. The ferry plunged underwater taking the last of the heavy water with it. Tragically, 26 passengers died. But Germany's experiments with the atomic bomb were finished.

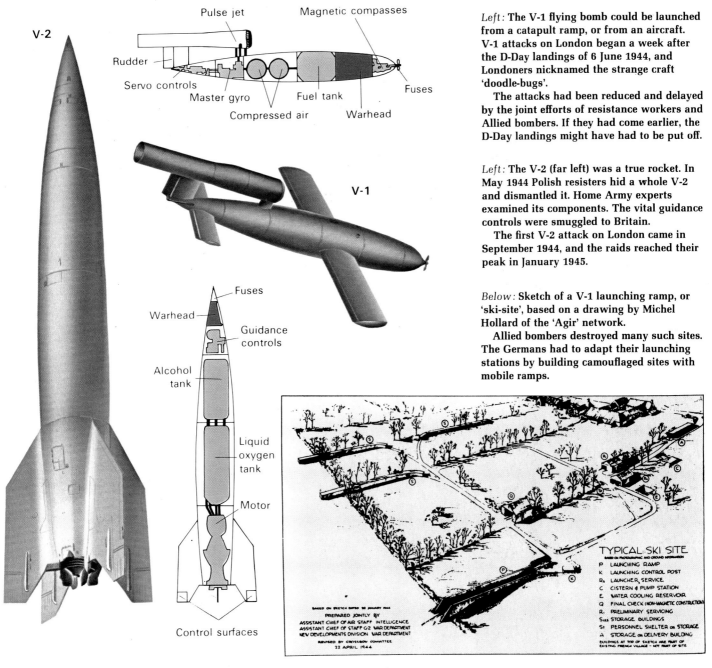

V-2

Pulse jet

Magnetic compasses

Rudder

Servo controls

Master gyro

Compressed air

Fuel tank

Warhead

Fuses

V-1

Fuses

Warhead

Guidance
controls

Alcohol
tank

Liquid
oxygen
tank

Motor

Control surfaces

Left: **The V-1 flying bomb could be launched from a catapult ramp, or from an aircraft. V-1 attacks on London began a week after the D-Day landings of 6 June 1944, and Londoners nicknamed the strange craft 'doodle-bugs'.**

The attacks had been reduced and delayed by the joint efforts of resistance workers and Allied bombers. If they had come earlier, the D-Day landings might have had to be put off.

Left: **The V-2 (far left) was a true rocket. In May 1944 Polish resisters hid a whole V-2 and dismantled it. Home Army experts examined its components. The vital guidance controls were smuggled to Britain.**

The first V-2 attack on London came in September 1944, and the raids reached their peak in January 1945.

Below: **Sketch of a V-1 launching ramp, or 'ski-site', based on a drawing by Michel Hollard of the 'Agir' network.**

Allied bombers destroyed many such sites. The Germans had to adapt their launching stations by building camouflaged sites with mobile ramps.

V-1 and V-2

In the winter of 1939, British intelligence discovered a secret German weapons project. It involved long-distance glider bombs and rockets, which had been unknown before. These were Hitler's 'revenge weapons', the V-1 flying bomb and V-2 rocket.

Polish slave labourers were being used to build a secret research station at Peenemünde in eastern Germany, and further information began to filter out through the Polish Resistance. Allied reconnaissance aircraft took blurred photographs of the base.

On 17 August 1943, 600 Allied bombers launched a mass raid on Peenemünde. It was only a partial success. The station was badly damaged, but certain vital areas remained intact.

Besides, work on the secret weapons was now going on elsewhere.

French resistance groups were discovering strange concrete structures being built at secret bases throughout northern France. They were shaped like long skis, and all pointed at London.

Again reconnaissance aircraft were called in. It soon became clear that the 'ski sites' were launching ramps for V-1s. The French 'Agir' network run by Michel Hollard discovered 79 sites; these were pinpointed for Allied bombers.

The RAF raided the sites in December 1943. German plans were delayed, and Hitler had to settle for much more modest V-1 attacks than he had intended.

By now, the Germans had moved their main V-2 works to a mountainous region of Poland, beyond the range of Allied

bombers. Here, they were building gigantic networks of underground tunnels and workshops, using slave labour from the concentration camps.

After one practice launch in May 1944, a V-2 landed off target near the River Bug. It failed to explode. Polish resistance workers raced to the site and hid the rocket in a swamp before the German search parties arrived.

Later, members of the Home Army returned to the spot, dug up the rocket and examined it in detail.

Their report, including all the important parts of the rocket itself, was smuggled out of Poland by Dakota aircraft and flown to England.

The Resistance could not stop the V-2 raids on London. But they did give advance warning of what to expect.

INVASION

D-Day

On 5 June 1944, a gigantic armada of warships and troop-carriers was gathered in England's Channel ports. That night, the BBC broadcast coded action messages to resistance groups in France. D-Day had arrived at last.

When dawn broke on 6 June, the Channel was black with ships of the biggest invasion fleet in history.

The air echoed to the thundering of guns. In a colossal struggle on the Normandy beaches, the Allies breached the German defences and gained a foothold on French soil.

French resistance groups started a massive campaign of sabotage. The aim was to disrupt communications and prevent the Germans from moving troops to the fighting front.

Railways, bridges and power stations were blown up. Telegraph and telephone lines were cut. Barricades and road-blocks were set up, and road signs painted black to confuse the Germans.

All the French groups now came under the command of de Gaulle's General Koenig, and were known as the French Forces of the Interior (FFI).

In some areas near the front, massed FFI forces faced the Germans in pitched battles. Elsewhere, groups of snipers unleashed volleys of gunfire on straggling German columns.

The Allies dropped massive supplies of weapons and explosives. Three-man teams of officers were parachuted in to co-ordinate plans, each consisting of an Englishman, a Frenchman and an American.

Above: **A bewildered SS officer surrenders to FFI men near Chartres, August 1944. The secret armies had been waiting for years for just such a day.**

Below: **FFI members clearing German vehicles from a road in Normandy to assist the Allied advance. Elsewhere, they were blocking roads to hinder the German retreat.**

Above: **A US paratrooper of 1944, armed with a Thompson M1A1 sub-machine-gun. In the early hours of 6 June, paratroopers were dropped behind German lines while the Allied invasion fleet set out for the Normandy coast.**

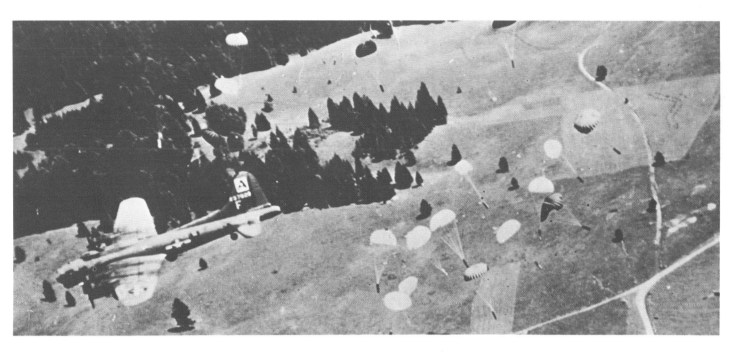

Disruption and reprisal

The hectic campaign of disruption had real effect. Thousands of German troops were pinned down in an attempt to keep order behind the fighting front.

One SS division struggling towards Normandy was held up time and again by sabotage, ambush and attack. When one of its commanders was shot dead by a sniper in one village, the SS took a ghastly revenge on a neighbouring village called Oradour-sur-Glane.

The male villagers were rounded up and shot dead. The women and children were locked in the village church which was then set ablaze. In all, 700 people were killed.

A few resistance groups seized territory and tried to hold it until the Allies arrived. But this only made sense near the fighting front.

Revolt

The Vercors plateau of southern France was far from the front. But the maquis rose in revolt, and 3000 resistance fighters declared the area a republic.

A German force four times their size advanced on the plateau, backed by artillery and aircraft. The rising was crushed with sickening violence.

A similar tragedy occurred in Eastern Europe, where the Russians were advancing through Poland. By late July, the people of Warsaw could hear the sound of Russian guns.

The Home Army rose, 40,000 strong, against their German oppressors. In two days they had seized much of the city, and Polish flags flew high again.

But outside the capital, the Russian advance had halted. Street by street the Germans managed to claw back the areas of Warsaw they had lost.

In weeks of savage street fighting, buildings crashed in ruins and the power supply was wrecked. Few supplies reached the rebels. The people of Warsaw began to starve.

At first, the free sections of the city managed to keep in touch with one another through the network of underground sewers. Then the Germans discovered what was going on, and the fighting spilled down into the tunnels.

The Home Army held out for over two months. But on 2 October the rebels had to surrender. By then, the historic city of Warsaw was a mass of rubble.

The Allies advance

Resistance groups were not equipped to withstand siege, as they had tried to do in Warsaw and the Vercors. They were most effective in hit-and-run actions co-ordinated with the Allied advance. And bit by bit, the Allies were driving the Germans back.

In Italy, Rome had fallen to the Allies. Mussolini, the country's Fascist dictator, had been ousted. About 300,000 freedom fighters had taken to the hills and were fighting as partisans to help the Allies.

Overall control of the partisans was held by a body called the CLN (national liberation committee). As the struggle progressed, the partisans began to liberate towns before the Allies reached them.

The Germans were fully extended on every front. But the war was not yet over.

Above: **A US aircraft drops canisters of supplies to the besieged Vercors plateau.**

The area had long been a maquis stronghold. But when it rose in open revolt, the Germans moved in in force. The Allies dropped weapons and supplies (on 14 July, the Americans dropped 1000 containers). The maquis held out for a few days of fierce cliff-top fighting before the Germans overran the plateau.

Above: **A postage stamp issued by the Polish Home Army during the Warsaw Rising. It is dated 1 August 1944. The letters AK stand for 'Armia Krajowa' (Home Army), and 'Poczta Polowa' means Field Post.**

It has been suggested that the Russians deliberately waited for the Germans to wipe out the rebels. The Home Army was a non-Communist body which might have caused them problems after the capital was liberated.

TENSION MOUNTS

Ambush and assassination

In August 1944, the Allies made a second landing in southern France. They were pressing in on Hitler's Europe from east and west, and struggling up through Italy in the south.

Assassinations increased. German soldiers rarely ventured out alone on country roads at night, and dark city streets could be just as dangerous.

After an attack it was vital to get rid of the body quickly. With luck, the Germans might believe that the victim had deserted, and so take no reprisals.

An American escape helper called Drue Tartière witnessed an assassination in Paris in broad daylight.

'Two young Frenchmen walked quickly past me. They were following a Nazi officer in front of them. As they passed me, they said something which sounded like "Now you'll see how we do it."

'Before I knew what was happening, one of them had stuck a knife between the shoulder blades of the Nazi officer, and before the Nazi could hit the pavement, the other had him by the seat of his pants and had hurled him into the Seine.'

On country roads, resisters might stretch wire between two trees to cut off the heads of approaching German motorcyclists. Another technique was to place three-headed nails in the path of a German vehicle to burst its tyres. SOE even invented explosive cowpats to halt vehicles in their tracks.

Ambushes often took place on hairpin bends, where enemy vehicles provided slow-moving targets.

In Crete, the German governor, General Kreipe, was ambushed. Two British agents, dressed as German soldiers, flagged down his car on a lonely bend in the road.

They knocked out the driver and spirited Kreipe away to a partisan hideout in the mountains. Later, the kidnapped general was smuggled out of Crete by submarine.

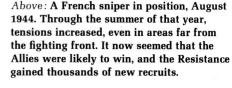

Above: **A French sniper in position, August 1944. Through the summer of that year, tensions increased, even in areas far from the fighting front. It now seemed that the Allies were likely to win, and the Resistance gained thousands of new recruits.**

Left: **A Russian poster captioned, 'One good turn deserves another'. In the first frame, a peasant is forced to doff his hat. In the next he becomes a partisan and a German is forced to doff his head.**
   The last Russian territories were liberated in August 1944.

Below: **A suspected collaborator is interrogated by resisters in Denmark. The liquidation of informers increased and collaborators were more and more isolated. They lived in terror of the midnight knock, the strangers at the door—and the fatal shots.**

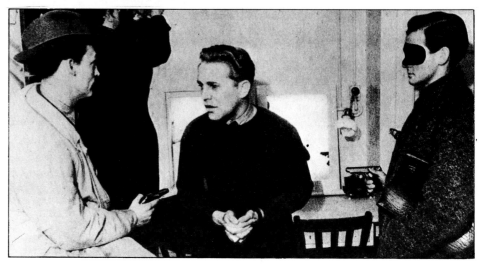

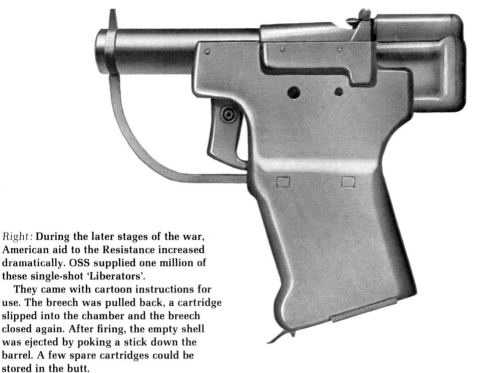

Right: **During the later stages of the war, American aid to the Resistance increased dramatically. OSS supplied one million of these single-shot 'Liberators'.**

They came with cartoon instructions for use. The breech was pulled back, a cartridge slipped into the chamber and the breech closed again. After firing, the empty shell was ejected by poking a stick down the barrel. A few spare cartridges could be stored in the butt.

Above: **The model of Copenhagen used by the RAF to brief pilots and navigators before the Shellhouse raid. The raid had been planned with great precision.**

The 18 Mosquitos were escorted by 28 Mustangs. They flew in low across the North Sea, crossing the coast at a chosen gap in the German anti-aircraft defences. **They swept over the countryside at tree-top height, and rushed in across St Jorgen's Lake.**

The first three planes bombed the Shellhouse (arrowed) almost at street level. The fourth hit a lighting mast, and disaster followed.

The July Plot

The prime target for assassination was Hitler himself. However, he was always well guarded. In Germany, Nazi control was so complete that it was hard for ordinary Germans to offer any active resistance at all.

But by July 1944 a group of German officers had become convinced that the war was lost and should be ended. They managed to plant a bomb at a conference which Hitler was attending.

The bomb went off. Hitler was badly shaken by the blast—but not killed. In revenge for the attempt, the Nazis murdered hundreds of suspected conspirators. The senior officers involved were strangled with piano wire and died dangling from meat hooks.

RAF raids

In 1944, the Nazi terror was so fierce throughout occupied Europe that in some places it threatened the very existence of organized resistance. The secret armies called for help from the Allies.

In February, RAF bombers raided Amiens prison to try to rescue various French resistance leaders.

Two months later, a bombing raid destroyed the Dutch population registry to hinder the Nazis' attempts to trace Jews and resisters.

In October, three squadrons of Mosquito bombers made a low-level attack on the Gestapo offices at the Aarhus in Denmark. Precision bombing destroyed the buildings where the Gestapo kept their files. As a bonus, 150 Nazi officers were killed in a conference hall.

In March 1945, a similar raid was launched against the Gestapo's Shellhouse building in Copenhagen. It was a tricky operation, because the Gestapo had deliberately moved their resistance prisoners to the upper floors.

Low-level bombing allowed most of the prisoners to escape from the blazing Shellhouse, and scores of the enemy were killed. The Resistance were also able to loot valuable Gestapo files.

By chance, however, most of the top Nazi officers were attending a funeral that day and so escaped. Worse, the fourth aircraft had hit a lighting mast and crashed near to a school.

Believing that the column of smoke was their target, some of the following planes showered bombs onto the school building. In the tragic blaze which followed, 86 Danish schoolchildren died.

LIBERATION

Right: **A Russian poster shows the Allied noose tightening around Hitler; Russia attacks from the East, Britain and the United States from the West. In April 1945, the three sides met on German soil.**

Below: **German troops surrender to FFI men in Paris. Gun battles broke out in the capital on 17 August. They lasted on and off through the following week. The formal German surrender came on 25 August 1944.**

Paris in revolt

In August 1944, the Allies were advancing through France, but Paris itself was still in German hands. The Allies did not want to storm the capital because of the suffering and devastation that were bound to follow. Instead, they decided to bypass the city and wait for the Germans to surrender it.

But freedom fighters in Paris felt differently. On 10 August the railwaymen went on strike. Five days later the police followed. Gun battles broke out. The police stormed their own headquarters and patriots occupied the town hall.

Paris was in revolt, and the Allied leaders began to fear a Communist takeover. The German commander had orders from Hitler to raze Paris to the ground rather than surrender it. But he could not bring himself to do it. Instead, he arranged a truce with the Resistance and withdrew his troops to a few strongpoints.

The people set up barricades with sandbags, cobblestones and whatever else came to hand. Soon fighting broke out again, and as it grew fiercer the Allies decided they had to send in troops after all.

On the evening of 24 August, the people heard the great cathedral bells of Notre Dame ringing continuously. An armoured division of Free French troops had reached the suburbs.

Street fighting went on overnight, but the next day the Germans surrendered. Parisians danced in the streets, girls showered kisses on the arriving troops and children played in the abandoned German tanks. Paris was free.

It was a time of joy, and of sorrow, too, for the 1500 Parisians who had died in the fighting. There were some ugly scenes as mobs took revenge against traitors and informers.

Women collaborators were shaved bald, marked with swastikas and paraded through jeering crowds. Many old scores were settled and inevitably some innocent people suffered.

Above: **Parisian girls embrace US troops as they drive through the capital. The Americans held a mass parade on 29 August, then moved on to pitched battle beyond the outskirts of the French capital.**

Above: **De Gaulle arrived in Paris on 25 August, and made his triumphal tour of the city centre the following day. Shots were fired as he entered Notre Dame, but the general was not hurt.**

Above: **A girl member of the Resistance helping to clear out the last groups of snipers from the capital. On 28 August, organized French resistance was officially dissolved; members could join the armed forces.**

Victory in Europe

Many civilian resisters now joined the Free French army and took part in the Allied drive towards Germany.

One by one, the other cities of occupied Europe were liberated: Brussels, Antwerp, Athens, Warsaw, Prague and Vienna. In April 1945, American and Russian troops met on German soil.

As the Reich disintegrated the Allies opened up the concentration camps and found scenes of appalling horror, where walking skeletons moved among the corpses of the dead, and typhus was rampant.

Among the human scarecrows who greeted the liberators were a number of resistance workers, including the Belgian escape helpers, Albert Guérisse and Andrée de Jongh. But many more had been shot in the last months.

On 30 April 1945, Hitler committed suicide in a Berlin bunker, and over the next few days all the remaining German armies surrendered. Victory in Europe was celebrated on 8 May.

There were street parties, parades and celebrations throughout Europe. But new tensions were emerging.

Aftermath

The Russians were tightening their grip on the countries they had overrun in Eastern Europe. Britain, France and the United States feared a new conflict. A 'Cold War' between East and West had emerged; it is still with us today.

In Greece, the Communist and non-Communist partisans fought on in a bitter civil war. It did not end until 1949, when the Communist partisans were crushed by the British and Americans.

But the evil of Nazism had been overthrown, and the Resistance had played a heroic part in the struggle. Many of its workers went on to become great national leaders: Tito and de Gaulle, for example.

After the war thousands of ordinary resisters simply returned to their normal jobs. Spies became railway clerks again, saboteurs returned to factory workbenches, and escape helpers went back to their farms.

Children who had once carried messages under the nose of the Gestapo returned to school, and national flags fluttered again from buildings where once the swastika had hung. The Nazi terror belonged to the past.

REFERENCE

Organizations

This list gives some of the main agencies and organizations working for and against the Resistance during World War Two.

Abwehr: the security and intelligence organization of the German armed forces.

BCRA (central bureau for information and action): the Free French secret service operating under de Gaulle's national committee.

Bopa (bourgeois partisans): nickname of a Communist-led subversive organization in Denmark.

CLN (national liberation committee): the leading anti-fascist body in Italy.

CNR (national council of the Resistance): the body set up by Jean Moulin to co-ordinate the resistance movements in France.

EDES (national republican Greek league): the main organization of the non-Communist partisans in Greece.

ELAS (Greek popular liberation army): the army of the Communist partisans in Greece.

FFI (French forces of the interior): a name applied to the French resistance groups from early 1944 onwards.

FTP (free-shooters and partisans): the fighting wing of the Communist resistance movement in France.

Gestapo (secret state police): the secret police force of Nazi Germany.

GRU (chief intelligence directorate): the military intelligence service of the Russian army.

Holger the Dane: a subversive group in Denmark, named after a legendary giant.

Home Army: the main non-Communist resistance organization in Poland.

MI 6: Britain's secret intelligence service (also known as SIS).

MI 9: Britain's secret agency dealing with escape and evasion.

Milorg (military organization): a secret body formed by Norwegian officers working in contact with their government-in-exile.

MIS-X: a secret American agency dealing with escape and evasion.

National Liberation Army: Tito's Communist partisan army in Yugoslavia.

NKVD (people's commissariat for internal affairs): the Russian state security, intelligence and subversion agency—a forerunner of the modern KGB.

Ordedienst (service for order): a right-wing Dutch resistance group working in contact with its government-in-exile.

OSS (Office of Strategic Services): the American secret service dealing with intelligence and subversion—a forerunner of the modern CIA.

PWE (Political Warfare Executive): a British agency set up to wage propaganda warfare.

RVV (resistance council): a left-wing Dutch resistance movement working in contact with its government-in-exile.

SD (security service): a Nazi body working against the Resistance.

Secret Army: a Belgian resistance movement working in contact with its government-in-exile.

SOE (Special Operations Executive): a British secret agency designed to encourage subversion in Europe.

SS (protection squad): a Nazi organization with many functions including working against the Resistance and manning the concentration camps.

Waffen SS: the armed force of the SS.

Further reading

General surveys
MI 9 M. R. D. Foot and J. M. Langley, The Bodley Head, 1979

Resistance M. R. D. Foot, Paladin Books, 1978

Resistance in Europe, 1939–1945 edited by Stephen Hawes and Ralph White, Allen Lane, 1975

SOE in France M. R. D. Foot, Her Majesty's Stationery Office, 1966

Illustrated surveys
The Partisans David Mountfield, Hamlyn, 1979

Secret Agents, Spies and Saboteurs Janusz Piekalkiewicz, David and Charles, 1974

Biographies (the names of the agents are given in brackets when they are not apparent in the titles)
Agent Extraordinary (Michel Hollard) George Martelli, Collins, 1960

Carve Her Name With Pride (Violette Szabo) R. J. Minney, Newnes, 1956

Little Cyclone (Andrée de Jongh) Airey Neave, Hodder and Stoughton, 1954

Madeleine (Noor Inayat Khan) Jean Overton Fuller, Gollancz, 1952

Nancy Wake Russell Braddon, Cassell, 1956

No Banners (the Newton Brothers) Jack Thomas, Allen, 1955

Odette (Odette Churchill) Jerard Tickell, Chapman and Hall, 1949

Six Faces of Courage (Moulin, Pilecki, Fourcade, Peulevé, de Jongh, Gerson) M. R. D. Foot, Eyre Methuen, 1978

They Came From The Sky (Cammaerts, Landes, Rée) E. H. Cookridge, Heinemann, 1965

The Way Back (Albert Guérisse) Vincent Brome, Cassell, 1957

The White Rabbit (Yeo-Thomas) Bruce Marshall, Evans, 1952

First-hand accounts
Codename Dora Sandor Rado, Abelard, 1976

Courage and Fear 'Rémy', Barker, 1950

Duel of Wits Peter Churchill, Hodder, 1957

The Embattled Mountain F. W. D. Deakin, Oxford University Press, 1971

The Great Game Leopold Trepper, Michael Joseph, 1977

Handbook for Spies Alexander Foote, Museum Press, 1949

The House Near Paris Drue Tartière, Simon and Schuster, 1946

Inside North Pole Peter Dourlein, Kimber, 1953

London Calling North Pole H. J. Giskes, Kimber, 1953

Maquis George Millar, Heinemann, 1945

Moondrop to Gascony Anne-Marie Walters, Macmillan, 1946

Noah's Ark Marie-Madeleine Fourcade, George Allen and Unwin, 1973

Of Their Own Choice Peter Churchill, Hodder, 1952

Portrait of a Spy 'Rémy', Barker, 1955

The Silent Company 'Rémy', Barker, 1948

Skis Against the Atom Knut Haukelid, Kimber, 1954

Special Operations Europe Basil Davidson, Gollancz, 1980

Spirit in the Cage Peter Churchill, Hodder, 1954

Ten Steps to Hope 'Rémy', Barker, 1960

We Landed by Moonlight Hugh Verity, Ian Allen, 1978

Who Lived to See the Day Philippe de Vomécourt, Hutchinson, 1961

INDEX

ACKNOWLEDGEMENTS

Key to picture positions
(T) top, (C) centre, (B) bottom, (L) left, (R) right, and combinations; for example (TR) top right.

Artists
Peter Acty 5, 11, 14, 15, 18–19, 27, 34, 35, 36–37, 38, 39, 43
Ron Hayward Associates 8, 21, 23, 30–31, 33, 40
Tony Payne 20

Photographs
BBC Hulton Picture Library 6(T), 22(B), 41(B)
Bundesarchiv 10(L), 12, 29(TL)
Comité d'Histoire de la Deuxième Guerre Mondiale/Institut d'Histoire du Temps Présent 21
Josef Garlinski/Methuen Paperbacks 37
Imperial War Museum 2, 6(C), 7(B), 8(L), 10(R), 16, 18, 35(B), 40(B), 41(T), 42(T), 43
Keystone Press Agency 9(TL), 20, 40(T), 45(B)
Librarie Academique Perrin, Paris/Methuen Paperbacks 34(L)
Librarie Arthème Fayard, Paris/Methuen Paperbacks 31

MacClancy Press 3, 4(T), 8(L), 9(CL), 11(TL), 24, 25, 27, 30(L), 42(B)
Peter Myers/Macdonald Educational Front cover, 6(B), 13(TL), 17(B), 26, 28(T), 43
Norges Hjemmefrontmuseum, Oslo 38
Novosti Press Agency 42(C), 45(T)
Ph. H. Noyer (©) A.D.A.G.D. 1981 7(T)
Photri 22(C), 44(BL), Back cover
Popperfoto 28(B), 36(T), 36(B)
Harry Rée 18
R.A.F. Museum, Hendon 32(T), 32(C), 33(C), 33(B)
Rijksinstituut voor Oorlogsdocumentatie/Charles Breyer 13(BL)
H. Roger-Viollet 11(TR), 44(T), 44(BR)
Snark International 24/25
Süddeutscher Verlag 14
John Topham Picture Library 23

From *M1 9* by M. R. D. Foot 32(B), 33(T)
From *Secret Agents, Spies and Saboteurs* by Janusz Piekalkiewicz 22(T), 39
From *The Way Back* by Vincent Brome 34(R)
From *Undercover; Codes and Ciphers* by Peter Way 29(R)

Editor: Lis Edwards
Designer: Tim Healey
Picture Research: Jenny Golden
Production: Rosemary Bishop

Front cover: Some items associated with the Resistance movement. Clockwise: a ration book and pass used in occupied Europe, a Colt 32 with bullets, a Rega Minox camera lying on a silk escape map, a Leica 3A camera and a Nazi armband.

Back cover: French patriots burning a portrait of Hitler.

© Macdonald & Co. 1981

First published 1981
Macdonald & Co. (Publishers) Ltd
Holywell House
Worship Street
London EC2A 2EN

ISBN 0 356 06553 7 (UK edition)
ISBN 0-382-06587-5 (US edition)

Printed and bound by
Purnell & Sons Ltd
Paulton, Avon, England